START TO EXIT

HOW TO MAXIMIZE THE VALUE IN YOUR START-UP

START TO EXIT

HOW TO MAXIMIZE THE VALUE IN YOUR START-UP

ADRIAN BURDEN

IN ASSOCIATION WITH:
*MALVERN FESTIVAL OF INNOVATION
AND THE GROWTH IDEA*

*For Emma, who has put up with me saying that
one day I will write a book. Well, here it is.*

Start to exit
How to maximize the value in your start-up

Published by Novaro Publishing Ltd, Techno Park,
Coventry University Technology Park, Puma Way, Coventry CV1 2TT

ISBN 978-1-9998329-0-2

British Library Cataloguing in Publication Data
A catatlogue record for this book is available from the British Library.

Cover designed by Ravina Patel
Typeset by Lawston Design

TABLE OF CONTENTS

- Sharing data on a server
- Staffing the departments
- Access privileges
- Sub-folders

9. Virtual is the new reality
- IT complexity
- Company email
- Data storage
- Remote access
- Disaster recovery
- Telephony
- Digital office
- Software tools
- Backing up across the team

10. Business agreements and disagreements
- Understanding what you are agreeing to
- A system for filing and tracking signed agreements
- Internal processes to handle agreements

11. Accounting the beans
- Watching the cashflow
- An accounting system that brings benefit
- Structure of company accounts
- Financial planning
- Staff expense forms
- Financial processes to smooth scale-up

12. Corporate branding and the style police
- Aiming for consistent branding
- Company logo
- A design guide
- Company stationery
- Web presence
- Policing your brand

- Company data
- Data servers
- Password protection
- Social media security
- Personal devices
- Remote data access
- IT systems management
- Disaster recovery

19. Sales close to the wind
- Generating revenue
- Quoting for sales
- Discounting and payment terms
- Overstretching the business
- Sales department knowledge
- Scaling sales quickly

20. Buttons, knobs and the dashboard
- In the cockpit
- Business instrumentation
- Third-party business software

21. Intellectual property rights (and wrongs)
- Imitation and flattery
- Intangible value
- IP protection
- Good practice
- Managing IP
- In-licences and sub-licences
- Counterfeiting
- Is IP everything?

22. Scale-up
- Corporate adolescence
- Scalable software systems
- Social responsibility
- Export

FOREWORD

This book is an ideal manual for ambitious entrepreneurs. It covers a huge number of subjects you will need to understand if you are creating a new enterprise, ranging from handling staff to choosing your name. The author is an ideal guide: he is an entrepreneur himself, and runs a business that incubates a number of growing companies. He is also the founder of The Malvern Festival of Innovation, a celebration of new ideas of technology held once a year in the Midlands spa town.

This book is different to many start-up business texts, because it covers the practical details. It is not a motivational self-help work: rather it is full of the nitty-gritty facts which you will need to know if your company is to be a success. Adrian's background is in science and technology, and it shows in his methodical approach to the various topics. He covers areas such as administration, IT, and legal matters especially well. These are the sort of dry but essential issues which can easily sink a business if the founder gets it wrong.

I would say that this is a book for the serious entrepreneur, who is determined to build a genuine firm with real potential. It shows how planning and proper organization in the early days can pay off in the long run – making sure legal agreements are documented, for example, and intellectual property protected. It is a comprehensive, easy-to-use reference for aspiring tycoons, and I thoroughly endorse its recommendations.

Good luck to every reader who takes the plunge and starts their own industrial empire.

Luke Johnson
Chairman, Centre for Entrepreneurs, the home of StartUp Britain,
Chairman, Risk Capital Partners LLP

INTRODUCTION: ON YOUR MARK

Panic on the start line

The first business I started was when I was living some 6700 miles from the country I called home. I vividly remember the evening a few days after I had spun off from a scientific research institute, having left a well-paid expatriate position to co-found a high-tech start-up called Singular ID. I had two children at an expensive international school, a significant monthly rent on an apartment, and had just heard the news that the business angel investor whom we had been courting for several months had announced it was too risky for him to invest after all. The air conditioning was not doing a very good job at keeping me cool, and outside it was approaching midnight in Singapore.

I felt tangible waves of panic and pondered what was now looking like an ill-conceived idea. The venture was indeed risky: we had a new but untested technology, a somewhat limited proof of concept, a couple of in-licensed patents pending, and still no customer. We did have the promise of some finance if we could find a third party to match it, but our remaining investor pipeline was not looking too promising. We had just signed a lease on a business premises and taken on an employee from the institute, as well as started paying for phones, utilities and intellectual property. I was already baulking at these liabilities and concerned that the joy of co-founding was in reality a misery of co-bankrolling an enterprise that had already broken the first rule of business: get a paying customer to prove a market need before doing anything else.

Fortunately, both my co-founder Peter and I were of similar mindsets: this was not going to be a job for life but rather an exercise in starting, growing and exiting a business in a timeframe measured in years rather than decades. We had both agreed it would be good to 'make a million', denominated in pounds sterling rather than the Singapore dollar, because at the time one needed about three million Singapore dollars for one million pounds sterling.

We also both agreed not to push our luck by continuously going back out for the next big wave: Peter had done quite a bit of surfing in his childhood and knew you could not always catch the wave you wanted because, one, the weather over which you had no control could change and, two, you eventually became too tired to ride the next wave properly anyway. We sensed the same applied to business; there was a lot we had no control over and we knew, already, we were going to find demands of entrepreneurship at times exhilarating but overall exhausting. As such, we both undertook to work hard but know when we should call time if things were going south, rather than throw more good money after bad.

And it was at this point, reflecting quietly to myself whilst staring at the patterns on the polished marble floor, that I mustered some courage and told myself: 'right, as there is no going back, we had better do this now, and we do it properly'. Because the mutually agreed aim was to grow controllably and sell lucratively as soon as conceivably possible, it followed that it was imperative to ensure everything in the business was structured with this in mind from the outset. As founding chief executive, I would make it my mission to implement systems, processes and strategies to exit the business through a trade sale as effortlessly as possible without over-encumbering our team or stifling creativity within the business along the way.

Why the book?

Since those cold sweats in hot Singapore, I have met many entrepreneurs starting out on a new business venture and almost none of them have the exit in mind. Great athletes see themselves crossing the finishing line first, before the starting gun sounds. I believe that great entrepreneurs should see a trade sale or a listing for their business in their mind's eye as they too are standing on their marks.

So, it is not my intention in this book to describe how to start and run a particular kind of business *per se*. There are plenty of books about this subject; the mechanics of forming a company, time-honoured ways to generate sales, methods to be great at marketing, best approaches to customer service, and so on. There are also lots of books by famous entrepreneurs describing their own exciting story and some of the lessons they learnt along the way.

Rather, I aim set out how to structure, operate and scale up a generic business with the future exit being the ultimate goal. Systemizing your business in this way brings real benefit to the general operations because it builds in resilience and gives everyone a clear goal. Being organized also makes it quicker and easier to secure financial investment along the way.

If you have picked this book up in the midst of growing your current business, that is fine as you will be able to tweak your existing structures and operations on the foundations you have already built. You will have an opportunity to review what you have already put in place and see if the processes are fit for purpose or if they can benefit from additional thought. Such self-analysis is always difficult when you feel you are fighting fires on a daily basis, but believe me that it is a lot easier before a potential investor or suitor comes calling (or to paraphrase: before a raging inferno takes hold).

Each chapter looks at one aspect of business foundation and growth. I will try to highlight certain pitfalls, offer solutions, and show you how a few simple precautions and processes that can be put in place early on will allow you to sleep at night, delegate more tasks to others, and give you the latitude to focus more strategically on the business. This is a virtuous cycle, as the more time you can be free to think creatively, the more likely your business will succeed. And to me, success for an entrepreneur is characterized as solid business growth followed by a trade sale or a stock-market listing; the exit.

Not everything that I describe will apply to every business, but some approaches used in one industry can be easily adapted for another sector and bring real benefit. A simple example of this crossover is the laboratory notebook. Used widely in research and development, because its numbered and signed pages help to provide a defensible record of invention, such an item is just as useful in an office-based start-up because it provides a record of when things were done and how your thinking developed. As such, let us call it a logbook.

There are also a few common threads that I have found run through the fabric of a growing business which I will try to highlight *en route*. For example, it is easy to spend money but some minor investments can be invaluable and far outweigh their actual cost in terms of the intangible benefit they provide

As Peter and I worked each day, we kept in mind the future warrants (promises) that we would have to make when we came to take on third-party investment or sell our business. I will point out some of things you will need to say, hand on heart, to give the potential acquirer comfort during their due diligence that they are buying a solid business and not a mirage. Lies, even those coloured white, will come back and bite you. If all your preparation lets you respond honestly to questions about your business and its operations, it brings ample rewards. If you sell your business and retire, you want to know that your relaxing years are secure and that you will not be facing a lawsuit a few years down the line. Having accurate information readily available at your fingertips will really help, as otherwise preparing for investment, a trade sale or a listing can be extremely time consuming and have a huge opportunity cost for your business at a crucial time.

Few people start more than one business in their lifetime, and those that do learn a lot for the second (or third) time around. Those of you embarking on the journey for the first time do not have the luxury of hindsight, so overall this book aims to give you a little secondhand hard-won experience.

And that is it really. I estimate you could read this book in perhaps four or five days and then you could work through all the actions in about two to three weeks with some concerted effort. Do this in the safe knowledge that it has taken me a lot longer to write it all down.

1.

ENTREPRENEURS GET SET, GO

Make the leap

There is no time like the present to bite the bullet and start a new business. I say this with conviction whether you are reading this in the depths of a financial depression or at the crest of a dotcom bubble. A recession may make it difficult to raise money, but you will probably find it easier and less expensive to hire first-rate people.

I also believe it whether you are young, free and single, a parent with a new family, or about to retire from the day job. If you are young you will have less to lose, but if you are older you will have years of experience under your belt to deal with some of the surprises you will encounter along the way in your new venture. It really does not matter. There are pros and cons with starting a business at any time of a financial cycle, or indeed at any time of your own particular stage of life. So, in my mind, anytime is a good time to make the leap.

I started my first business in Singapore with two young children in primary school. I had already worked in the UK as an employee in another technology start-up and seen firsthand the stresses that the founders had to endure, so to some extent I went in with my eyes open. Over time the cons became apparent in that I was having to travel frequently long haul to Europe and the United States spending time away from my wife and children. My co-founder Peter and I also had to work early and late on phone calls with potential customers and investors in different time zones. None of this activity is good for a family life, but the pros of having made a start and being focused on the exit became apparent with time. The eventual trade sale brought financial gain that has since enabled our family to enjoy living in our ideal house in a lovely part of England. It took many sacrifices to get there, but the exit was what made it all worthwhile.

The key point therefore, and indeed the subject of this book, is to make the leap in a controlled fashion. Do not just shut your eyes and hope you land on your own two feet, but rather jump so that you hit the ground running in the direction you wish to travel. How you start and grow your new business at the outset could have a real impact on how easy it is for you to finance, sell or, indeed, publicly list your company a few years down the line. Ideally, you want your first steps to already be in the direction marked exit. Even if you do not get it all right from the word go, being able to correct and adapt early on will be of great benefit later.

Personal and business

The first thing I did was to separate my personal life from my new venture. This was largely a psychological step, but one worth taking. A start-up is an all-encompassing and all-absorbing project, and it will quite simply 'mess with your head' unless you define a few boundaries and erect a few firewalls.

But it is also a physical step, so, wherever possible, I recommend using separate online accounts and subscriptions (such as email, social media) and also separate assets (for example, a computer, tablet or phone) in your business from your personal ones. The reason is, even if you are starting out as a home-based business, keeping business life and all that goes with it separate will make it so much easier later as you scale up and exit.

If you do use personal effects such as your own email address to get going, keep a record of where they have been used, so that you can migrate across to company ones once they are in place.

Your first asset: the logbook

Take a step back and jot down on the back of an envelope your business idea, your aims and your objectives. What is the idea? Will you be making a product or offering a service? Will you need much money to get it going and if so where will it come from? What is your ultimate aim: fame, fortune or a comfortable life?

Actually, it is best not to use the back of an envelope. These tend to get lost. Yet this is a critical stage in your new business. It is probably the first articulation of your new business plan; possibly the first time you are defining the scope in black and white. You could write these thoughts on your computer, but I would recommend simply using a new hard-backed notebook and writing this on the first page; this is your logbook. Even if you are not starting a technology-based company, you are embarking on some research and development for your new venture, so the same discipline will apply.

There is something invigorating about writing with ink in a new notebook that is commensurate with starting a new venture: remember the start of George Orwell's *1984* and how Winston Smith relished writing his first few words in his new diary? And, just like you were taught at school, do write the date in the margin.

Now you have it. A date-stamped record of your new business idea on paper. It may be a bit sketchy or it may already be detailed. It will certainly miss out some important hitherto unknown points, but already your mind is clearing and you can start to see wood for trees. This is the beginning of your all-important business plan. The discipline of having committed thoughts to paper comes naturally to some, harder to others, but I consider it a crucial first step. Do not worry, not everything will be on paper in this way; I am an advocate of using technology, but there are a few things that I believe should be handwritten like this. There is still a place for the humble notepad even if it is mainly filled with doodles. But yes, you could use an iPad or Galaxy Note if you prefer.

Exit warrant

Just be sure at this stage that your business plan and your product or service idea isn't someone else's. I have come across several entrepreneurs who have started their own company and poached some of the ideas from their previous employer. It would be a shame to put a lot of effort into something only to be served a lawsuit saying you stole the idea whilst working for another company. Hand on your heart that no-one else has a claim to the intellectual property you are about to use or develop?

Your logbook will also be a key company asset. It may not have much financial value, but the intellectual value will gradually increase as you complete the pages. Therefore, it would be wise and useful to number it. Rather than call it 'book 1', let us start the asset register now and adopt a simple scheme and label it AN0001. If there are more than one of you (co-founders), each should get a book labelled AN0001, AN0002 and so on.

It may seem a little early to be labouring the point of labelling assets, but I vividly recall a conversation with one of our investors in Singapore after they had completed our first significant round of finance. He recounted how they had seen the asset labels on our notebooks during a meeting and this was one of the reasons why they were comfortable investing. To them it showed that we were organised and took the value of our intellectual property seriously. So, a small detail can sometimes clinch a deal.

Invaluable capex: a hardback notebook

It sounds a bit retrograde, but a hardback notebook can be a useful thing. I prefer A4 in size, but maybe A5 could be good too. Best to choose one size and stick with it for the course. Choose one with strong sewn bindings (not loop bound) and ideally one with page numbers. This can help you keep a record of all your ideas. In fact, it is so important, I suggest you label the first one as an asset AN0001. And why not buy five at the start so you have them ready to give other staff as they come on board? Outlay about £5-£25.

Early on is also the time to start an Asset Register. To begin with you can just keep a physical list on a piece of paper or an electronic list on a computer spreadsheet. The point is to start the register so that it can be migrated later to a more versatile system. So, at this stage you will have something simple a little like Figure 1.1.

Asset register

AN	Date added	Item	Holder	Location	Date disposed
0001	YYYYMMDD	Logbook	Your name	Your office	
0002	YYYYMMDD	Logbook	Co-founder	Their office	
0003					

Figure 1.1. The start of the company asset register and the two logbooks that now form the company's first assets.

Why all the fuss?

Traders have been setting up corner shops, service outlets and other enterprises for hundreds of years. There have been entrepreneurs since the year dot, so what has changed that makes systemizing a business important?

I think a key development in recent times is that there are more technology-based businesses going beyond simply buying and reselling or manufacturing and selling. There are also fewer large companies and organizations offering jobs for life and many more smaller businesses operating in a far greater variety of niches. Finally, things are moving very quickly and so in general to be successful you will need to keep up to date with not just new technology, but also new legislation and a global market place with a diverse range of rules, regulations, and cultures. Entrepreneurs need to be polymaths, or at least know enough people to seek answers quickly to a broad range of questions in a wide range of disciplines. This activity all takes time and effort. The smoother your operation, the more opportunity for the management team to cope with the modern demands on a growing business.

I once met someone who said he knew enough about a subject to be dangerous. This was an interesting remark, as there comes a point where you know sufficient about something to convince yourself you know enough to get by, yet you could be quite ill-informed and easily make the wrong decision. It is a balancing act; the need to be a Jack of all trades and yet a master not of none, but of some.

The overarching solution is to accept complexity and systemize processes wherever possible. You will want your business to be fathomable by a potential successor despite the fact that as it grows, it becomes more complex and demanding.

No time like the present

Finally, my biggest piece of advice at this stage is: action this day. I hear so many people talk about starting a business. I once had an academic tell me that they were dead set on spinning off a technology business from a university but that he needed to be really sure the chosen idea would work first, because he could not afford for it to be the wrong one. In fact, he may never know. Doing it will tell you, and bending your legs ready to make the leap is far better than sitting down to reflect. I looked him up again recently, nearly two decades after the conversation, and guess what? Still at the same university, but up a few notches on the pay spine.

So, as you embark on your entrepreneurial journey, do not find an excuse to vacillate and contemplate. Start-ups benefit hugely from being small and agile, so do what you can today, and do not put it off until tomorrow.

Take-away and to-do list

- First-cut articulation of what you want to do, will do or are doing.

- Firewall between your working life and personal life.

- Label assets from the word go in a simple, scalable manner.

- Start today, not tomorrow.

☑ tick them as you do them

☐ Labeled asset AN0001 and possibly AN0002

☐ Started an asset register

2.

LIFESTYLE BUSINESS OR LIFE-DEFINING?

The broad spectrum of businesses

One of the first things to think about is the nature of your business. There are a number of broad categories into which it may fall, each in my view requiring successively more effort and posing more risk. As I am a scientist by training, I realised that this gradation of complexity (and, therefore, the exertion required) can be usefully overlaid on the visible light spectrum ranging from the relatively low energy red end to the higher energy violet end of the rainbow.

Firstly, there is the lifestyle business. Using the analogy above, this type of business sits firmly at the low-energy infrared end. The lifestyle business is, after all, supposed to be relatively easy-going; generating income by doing something that is hopefully enjoyable to you nor over-demanding on your time. This category is where you see the business as a means of funding your future without necessarily growing to take over the world. The danger with this philosophy is that you are lulled into a false sense of security and do not structure your business for growth or an exit. After all, even a lifestyle business may need to be sold or at least passed on to your descendants.

Exit warrant

It is well worth being clear about the type of business from the start to position it for the eventual exit. Even a lifestyle business may progress to a lucrative exit. When it does, all the company assets (tangible and intangible) will go with it. A pitfall with the lifestyle business is that it becomes very entwined with your personal life (personal contacts, family members as employees, shared resources with the home, and so forth). Try to keep these things separate from the outset so that when you come to sell, you are selling your business, not your family heirlooms.

The next in line is a franchise where you license another brand and use it to leverage your own venture. This can, and indeed should, bring along with it a strong ready-made foundation such as templates and structures, courtesy of the franchise owner. This type of business is also more difficult to position for a sale because you are reliant on the franchise. However, you can still grow a franchise business successfully, then sell it on within the terms of the franchise; after all they will want a successful franchisee to continue trading successfully when you want to move on or retire. Before you take on a new franchise, look into the exit clauses and see if other entrepreneurs have successfully sold within the constraints of the scheme. Moreover, you will want to be sure that they are an organized business themselves and have thought about how their own enterprise grows in an orderly manner adopting the best practices from across their network.

A plain-vanilla consultancy is positioned around the orange part of the spectrum; and by consultancy I mean many aspects of service provision such as accountancy, legal services, estate agency, technical consultancy, and so forth. Such businesses may demand plenty of continuous professional development on a personal level to stay up to date with legislation and sector developments, but from a business perspective things are relatively straight forward. There will be some sales and marketing processes to manage without the support of a franchise; human resources will likely be the area of highest cost and greatest management time; and the company builds value on its reputation and performance. These kinds of businesses may not be highly scalable (they tend to rely on a proportionate number of people to the revenue potential because much of what is being done relies specifically on human resource), but they are highly saleable. As I write, there are plenty of examples in my neighbourhood where legal and accountancy businesses are consolidating into larger jointly-owned entities, so if you build a solid client base this can be a good route to eventual exit.

The UK is often referred to as a nation of shopkeepers, but in my view these types of businesses are actually fairly complex. Effectively a reseller, such enterprises rely on sound product knowledge, as well as the ability to monitor stock, deal with logistics, process returns and even offer online e-commerce options. So, I place the shop in the yellow region of the spectrum, whether it is a physical retail outlet that requires facilities management or a virtual shop which requires good IT management and the fulfillment of orders from a distance. Running a café, bar or restaurant also falls into this category, except that there is an element of production (in the form of meal preparation) to consider.

Middle of the road, in the green region of the spectrum, lies the systems integrator; offering specialist knowledge to create and install systems comprising products that work well together. All the skills and attributes we have already discussed apply along with some technical competence to source, deliver and support bespoke options effectively. Now you will need an able technical team to manage aspects of product customisation and implementation. Processes will necessarily be more complicated, and your employees likely to be more broadly skilled and having a variety of job functions as you grow. And do not just think about technology businesses here, because household plumbers and electricians are systems integrators as well.

Once a business starts to manufacture products, so the complexity really increases. Sitting squarely in the higher energy blue region are, I believe, software companies. Their virtual products do not require much capital equipment to create, but they do need stage gates to specify, code, support and deliver. This applies equally to web applications, mobile applications and software as a service (SaaS). This type of business is also highly scalable and can grow across the globe relatively quickly. Doing so adds complication in customer support, language support and dealing in different legal jurisdictions.

Manufacturing physical products, including traditional items like furniture and food, are in the high energy part of the spectrum; shades of blue and indigo. Why? Because the business needs to deal with the bill of materials, a supply chain, the production process, all the associated quality control, warehousing and delivery logistics. As the enterprise grows, along come warranty returns, export controls and worldwide distribution networks. This is all tricky and demanding stuff requiring diverse skills, fantastic management, facilities housing equipment and plenty of resources.

So, what can possibly be worse and sit at the ultraviolet end of the spectrum? Well that would be the high-tech start-up. It is all of the above with specialist knowledge, research and development (R&D) unknowns, patents and venture capital thrown in. The business needs to handle an element of technical R&D, a product development pathway, a production process with quality control and change control, and a support team for technical customers. These activities bring with it intellectual property protection, more complicated end-user agreements and license agreements, warranty issues and greater public liability. If executed well, the business can also grow to become a very valuable and sellable entity.

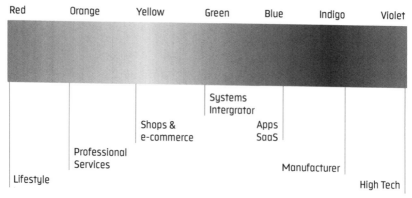

Red	Orange	Yellow	Green	Blue	Indigo	Violet

Systems
Intergrator

Shops &
e-commerce

Apps
SaaS

Professional
Services

Manufacturer

Lifestyle

High Tech

Figure 2.1. Classifying the complexity of different categories of business using the analogy of the visible light spectrum from low-energy red to high-energy violet.

There are, of course, many businesses that fall between these broad categories, and you would be right to argue that some businesses are much more complicated than others. I have not, for example, included the running of a hotel, a workshop or a dental surgery, and I only alluded to a café or restaurant in passing. However, the point is to think through where your business sits and the complexity that it may present as you start and grow. The more of the overall business process that you can anticipate at the start, the easier it will be to keep things under control moving forward.

Think through where your business 'notion' (note how I have not used the word 'plan' yet) lies on the spectrum of complexity and be prepared to handle all the different aspects that the venture will present. Anything other than a lifestyle business will put huge demands on your brain, your time, and potentially your bank balance, so be sure your partner and/or family have bought into the venture as well.

Before I co-founded Singular ID, I had worked in a display technology start-up in Oxfordshire. This really opened my eyes to the complexities of a high-technology start-up because the team of scientists needed to grow quickly to meet the milestones being set by the venture capitalists who were pumping in the money. Fast-growing teams are necessary because there is a narrow window of opportunity in which to bring a new technology to market, but fast-growing teams are also extremely difficult to manage effectively.

Location

The issue of physical (or virtual) location of your venture is also worth some consideration at this early stage. Firstly, a business needs a registered address where, at least in principle, its company books can be viewed at request. It is also a reliable address where authorities can reach you in writing to inform you of specific requirements or deadlines like filing tax or company information. The registered address can, of course, be your home, but it is usually better not to impinge on your private life. Choose your accountant's office, your solicitor's office or a local business centre if possible (always getting their permission first, of course). This will also ensure that mail reaches you even if you move house or go on holiday, especially if the address used offers a mail-opening service so as to screen the correspondence and check nothing is urgent.

The business address (where your activities by and large take place) and/or your correspondence address can be different from the registered address. But, again I would recommend that you avoid using your home address if at all possible unless you really are going to be a home-based business. Some businesses also generate large quantities of physical mail, especially those selling goods online. Unless a warehouse is fulfilling your orders, you will be processing stock replenishments, dispatches and returns all from this address.

The other consideration of a business addresses is that it can be troublesome to change, so try to choose a location that will have some future. Remember all the appropriate authorities, your suppliers (including your bank), your customers and all your marketing collateral (like business cards, leaflets, letterheads, compliments slips, and so forth) will feature your address. Change it too often, and you will be bogged down with all the associated bureaucracy of redrafting and reprinting whilst missing out on customer orders and sales opportunities.

Invaluable capex: the value of not spending

The good news is that starting and growing a company does not have to cost a lot of money all of the time, and if you can spend some time thinking, you will not necessarily be spending cash. No outlay.

Location can also create the right image for your business and any visitors to your premises. Having a business location inspires confidence. Meeting in a coffee shop, after a while, does not. Even if you decide to work from home the majority of the time, having a hot-desk or virtual office somewhere nearby can provide a venue for meetings, a location for customer correspondence, and a place to head to when the sight of your own wallpaper makes you want to quit.

When I co-founded the business in Singapore, we chose to start out in a glitzy new development called the Biopolis. The incubator in which we rented a unit was a little more expensive than some of the older properties in the neighbouring industrial estates, but the clean modern facilities resonated with our high-tech business. When we had visits from potential investors, customers and collaborators, you could tell instantly that they liked the surroundings and considered that we must be a viable, successful and ambitious business.

However, importantly at the start, you will want low rental overheads and flexible terms in the agreement for the facilities you use. At this stage, you will need to be sure that the services you subscribe to can be easily undone or upgraded as your business evolves. In fact, this seemingly minor aspect of business had quite a bit of impact on me.

I have since co-founded and run a serviced business centre that hosts other start-ups and small medium enterprises in Malvern, a small rural town in the west of England. We called the building an innovation centre to give the address some cachet and we made some effort to ensure the rental agreements have relatively simple, easy-in-easy-out terms with as much included as possible within a fixed monthly price. This is so that the entrepreneurs can worry about their business and not the itemised costs of hiring a boardroom, paying for cleaning, paying the UK's tiresome business rates or sorting out waste and recycling contracts. In your own property, these factors can be a huge distraction from your real business operations. So, in summary, aim to outsource or delegate the routine business premises matters so that you do not have to worry about them day to day.

Another consideration for the address is if the location is in a region (such as a district or county) that will benefit from local, regional, national or (in the case of the UK and Brexit notwithstanding) European grants. Deprived areas, areas with existing industry clusters, and regions with particularly proactive local councils or enterprise organisations can offer funding opportunities that neighbouring regions may not.

Once you are ready with your address it is time to start the company information document that will be the seminal record of all the business information that you start to generate. This means that you will have a written version of the correct full address to be used by all staff on all documents and collateral in the future. It may seem a bit pedantic, but it is surprising how often a company's details can vary between one item to another because there is not a central record to refer to. This will also form a useful staff induction document in the future.

The company information document, as illustrated in Figure 2.2, should start with a document number and a version number. Without too much explanation at this point, I'm going to refer to it as DN0001.1. This is your first company document, so has the enviable document number (hence the acronym DN) of 0001, the leading zeros offering some useful future proofing to the format. It is also, at this moment in time, in its first version; hence the '.1'.

Company information DN0001.1	
Registered address	Start to Exit, Wyche Innovation Centre, Walwyn Road, Malvern WR13 6PL, United Kingdom
Correspondence address	Start to Exit, Wyche Innovation Centre, Walwyn Road, Malvern WR13 6PL, United Kingdom

Figure 2.2. The master record of company details as they are confirmed.

Take-away and to-do list

- Businesses span a range of complexity.

- Categories of businesses in increasing complexity are: lifestyle, franchise, consultancy, retail, systems integrator, software developer, physical product manufacturer, high-tech start-up.

- Think carefully about the physical location (registered address, correspondence address and place where the operations will largely take place). Using your home address is not the best choice, even for a lifestyle business.

☐ Understood the type of business being embarked on and its complexity.

☐ Identified a registered office, correspondence address and/or business address for your business.

☐ Started a company information document, referenced as DN0001.1.

3.

MISSION, VISION AND ALL THAT JAZZ

Top-level goals ahead of the business plan

Like the universal acceptance of well-known brands of fast food, businesses the world over have adopted the American way of attaching a mission statement, a vision statement, core values, value proposition and so on to a business.

Usually these sentences get crafted well down the line when the business is jaded and frankly in need of a good shake-up. I am not a great fan of these terms, but they do serve a few purposes, and given that you might need them, best to get them sorted early on. You can always change them later with an expensive management consultant and a few days of senior management meetings, but hopefully you will have made a polite exit by then.

So, given that you probably do have an idea of what you do (or want to do) as a business, it is worth jotting down a few keywords around this and trying to make a reasonably coherent sentence or two. Use your logbook for this, as when you are rich and famous, these will be valuable musings for your charitable foundation to showcase in their archive centre. Or, failing that, it will be interesting for you to browse through and wonder where it all went wrong.

Vision

The vision statement is where you want your business to be sometime in the future. It is supposed to be a loosely realistic but stretch target, something like 'the world leader in...' or the 'first choice for...'. Keep it snappy and keep it understandable in layman's terms. You will be able to use this in your business plan and on your website. Your articulated vision should also be something that will motivate you and your future staff around the world. Think big, but do not make it something that will make employees or customers squirm.

Mission

The mission statement is what you do day-to-day, ideally hinting at what it is that makes you different from others around you. Again, keep it succinct and readable so that it can be understood by both potential investors and your customers. And make sure it will resonate with your staff too, as they are your team on the mission. Examples would be things like 'to provide the most reliable and cost effective...' or 'to do this and that well to help with the other'.

Core values

Core values are just attributes that make you and your organization tick and so are likely to be good things to build your business around. Think a little about the market you will be in, and what customers would benefit from: trustworthiness or security, valuing people's views, being quick to respond, being sustainable or environmentally responsible, and so on. Aim to have five or six key adjectives and then write a sentence about each to encapsulate what you mean when they are applied to your business.

Choose things you believe in, as you are the one going to build your business. Do not harp on about being environmentally friendly if you do not recycle at home, unless you have had an epiphany and are about to change your ways.

In terms of the company I co-founded that provided anti-counterfeiting products and services to help protect brands from pirated goods, here is what we came up with fairly near the beginning of it all. Our vision was: 'to be the leading solution provider for tracing and authenticating items of value'. And our mission was: 'to safeguard our customers' interests by providing integrated tagging solutions that protect people, brands, corporate images and market share'.

Invaluable capex

Writing down a motivating mission and an inspiring vision can be assisted by reading about other entrepreneurs who started out small but built global businesses. You could source a few to read (do not put this book down yet). A few suggestions are:

Against the Odds: an Autobiography, James Dyson

Losing my Virginity: the Autobiography, Richard Branson

What you see is what you get: my Autobiography, Alan Sugar

If you buy some or all of these books, you have just started your company library which other staff will be able to browse and borrow from in the future. Add some asset labels to these books too: AN0003, AN0004, etc. Use your local library and then there will be no financial outlay.

Value proposition

The value proposition is what you (will) do for your customers that (will) make them, hopefully, keep returning to you for more products and services. Often this starts out centering around an invaluable offering that people will simply not be able to do without. But you know that this manna from heaven does not come often, and really you need to be a bit more analytical about whether it will save someone time or money compared to what they do now.

Exit warrant

Firstly, be sure you stay on mission, honour your core values and strive for your vision. Filing away one or two examples to illustrate that you have indeed done so for future reference (like a customer testimony or a press release relating to a milestone) is a useful exercise. Acquirers will like this even though they will almost certainly want to change your mission, vision and core values as soon as they can to align with their own thinking. Do not be too offended by this, but rather embrace their curiosity and feign interest to facilitate changes as soon as the deal is done.

Definitive version

Once you have the statements, add them to your company information document, as shown in Figure 3.1. so that the definitive wording is captured on your hymn sheet and everyone in the business can start singing from the same one.

Company information DN0001.1	
Registered address	. . .
Correspondence address	. . .
Mission	To provide relevant and useful insights and procedures to help you maximize the value in your start-up.
Vision	To be the leading resource on shaping your start-up business so that it is ready for an exit.

| Core values | Reader-focused (readable prose with accessible text and well laid-out information), Actionable (providing information and ideas that can be implemented for immediate and long-term benefit), Respect (for the readership's own experience, limited time and limited money). |
| Value proposition | A relatively low-cost resource available in print and electronic form that can be read in bed or used as a workbook on the job. |

Figure 3.1. The company information document now includes definitive statements of mission, vision, core values and value proposition.

So, there. You have done it without spending a fortune with a consultant and, hopefully, you have distilled your ideas into a few structured sentences that describe what you (will) do (your mission statement), why what you do is valuable (your value proposition), where you want to be in the future (your company's vision), and how you will achieve it following a certain set of ideals (the core values). If for no other reason, potential investors will like these, and if your statements even partly resonate with a potential suitor when the time comes, they could help you clinch a trade sale too.

Take-away and to-do list

- A vision, mission and short list of core values should be concise, believable and not cringeworthy.

- A value proposition is what you bring to the table that differentiates you from the next punter.

☐ Vision statement crafted

☐ Mission statement crafted

☐ Set of core values agreed

☐ Value proposition understood

☐ Company information document updated

4.

BUSINESS IDENTITY: WHAT'S IN A NAME?

Company name

If you have not got one already, you need a name for your company. Usually the business idea comes first. Hopefully, the exercise of creating vision and mission statements may also have helped in the quest for an identity. The name more often than not describes the business or main offering in some way. However, sometimes the name is nothing much to do with the product, such as Apple. Occasionally the name is a made-up word such as Google (itself derived from the mathematical term googol which is a very large number). But for names to become as well-known as these examples takes a lot of time, money, luck and effort. Brands have to be built, which is easier when the name is descriptive, simple and/or memorable.

You will need to say your company name to people over the phone, at meetings, and whilst pitching in the elevator. Make sure your choice is spelt how it sounds to avoid confusion, and that it is easy and unambiguous to pronounce.

Once you have a contender, you need to make sure the company name is available. You can check Companies House (www.companieshouse. co.uk) or other national registrars when you are starting or planning the business. Search around the proposed name to make sure it is not too close to something else. Also, with business being a global pastime these days, you probably do not want to impinge on another company in another key country either. It is not easy to check this kind of thing exhaustively, but looking for domain names is a good start.

Check a domain with a service provider such as EUKhost (www. eukhost.co.uk), GoDaddy (www.godaddy.com) or 123Reg (www.123-reg.co.uk). If your business is going to be global, I think that you really need to have the dot com. You do not want prospective customers in the future heading by default to the dot com if it is not you. Check similar spellings or the use of hyphens between words. Finally, you may want to register several related domains, such as .com, .co.uk (if you are a UK-based business) and .biz. Checking these variants for your potential use is also a good way to find products, services and organizations in other countries using your proposed name.

Sometimes, names that are close to existing ones can cause issues. I remember as a child hearing about a London shop called British Gnome Stores. They made the national news because British Home Stores threatened to close the business if they did not rebrand. More recently, Instagram kicked up a fuss about a new UK app, Littergram, which aimed to cut rubbish on the streets through photography. Such are the complications of a business identity.

Our anti-counterfeiting business in Singapore was called Singular ID. It came about because we wanted some national buy-in for in-licensing and government grants, and I knew there were companies like Singapore Technologies, Singtel (the phone service provider), SingPost (the postal service) and so on, so I looked up words beginning with 'Sing'. Singular was spot on because it, of course, refers to 'one' (and we were developing a technology that gave individual items a unique identity) as well as having another meaning around being 'the best'.

Interestingly, one potential investor who was also in the intellectual property business expressed concern that Singular ID was too close to the US telecoms provider Cingular that was growing at the time. We thought about it, but our double-barrelled name in a different sector with a different spelling seemed sufficiently different for us to stick with it, and we did. Cingular soon became part of AT&T, so it never became a problem for us anyway.

The consultancy company I later co-founded is called Key IQ. The similarity in construct (IQ instead of ID) is I think a coincidence, as this brand came about because we wanted a short name that referred to 'crucial intelligence' or 'important insight'.

Doing your homework first is important because you really do not want to be compelled to change your name in the future. Then again, choose a good name and you could sell it. In 1999 a spin-out from Oxford University called Nanox changed its name to Oxonica early in 2001, selling the name Nanox to the UK company Elementis for a six-figure amount. Nanox is now a registered trademark for a chemical product.

Short-form company code

Once you have your company name, I find it useful to come up with a short form that can be used internally as a code. For example, My Company Ltd could have a code MyCo. Something four to six letters in length that can be pronounced or enunciated is ideal, but do not feel too constrained if you want to use fewer or more letters. However, the short form will be regularly used as an identifying prefix, so do not make it too long or too vague.

I am currently closely involved with three companies; Key IQ Ltd (KEYIQ), Innovate Malvern CIC (InnoM) and UK Cyber Security Forum CIC (UKCSF). Using prefixes like this is even more useful if you have more than one company on the go, as not only do you know which one you are referring to, but they are all kept separate within the overall system.

Furthermore, there is a possibility that you will expand your business overseas as well, so it is well worth starting a scalable system early on. Therefore, add a postfix GB (if you are starting or headquartered in the UK). If you are in another country, select the appropriate two-letter code listed by the International Organization for Standardization (ISO). I will use CC to mean country code in the nomenclature going forward, although in reality this is the code for the Cocos (Keeling) Islands.

You will recall that we labeled our first asset AN0001, and you may have labelled a few more items since. To bring this system under our latest scheme, you should go back and add the prefix so that the first item is referred to as MyCo-CC-AN0001. This means an asset is instantly recognizable as being associated with the specific company in the appropriate jurisdiction or territory. This is a useful scheme even if you only have one company, as it future proofs you should that situation change. It is also beneficial in a co-working space where you will be able to keep track of your company's belongings. So now your asset register and accompanying asset labels should be something like that shown in Figure 4.1, with the colour blue highlighting changes and additions from what you had earlier.

My Company Ltd Register of assets					
MyCo-CC-ANxxxx					
AN	Date added	Item	Holder	Location	Date disposed
0001	YYYYMMDD	Logbook	Your name	Your office	
0002	YYYYMMDD	Logbook	Co-founder	Their office	
0003					

Figure 4.1. Updated asset register and associated labels to include a short form for the company name and territory details.

Invaluable capex

You can save a lot of time labelling assets with a low-cost label printer, which becomes useful in future for labelling physical files, folders and dividers. It can also be used to professionally address envelopes if you are sending lots of letters or shipping products. A good example is the Dymo LabelWriter 450 which plugs into a USB socket on your computer. And the great thing is that you can use the label printer to label itself as an asset. £75 outlay + label stock.

In a similar way, the top of your company information document can also be updated to reflect this enhanced naming convention, and also to include the chose company name, as illustrated in Figure 4.2.

My Company Ltd Company information	
MyCo-CC-DN0001.1	
Company name	My Company Ltd
Registered address	. . .
Correspondence address	. . .
Mission	. . .
Vision	. . .
Core values	. . .
Value proposition	. . .

Figure 4.2. Updated company information document.

Also, with this short-form naming system now in place, you can create a document register that follows a similar logic to the asset register, so that you can keep track of the latest versions of important documents. Starting this on a simple spreadsheet is fine, as it can always be migrated to a more sophisticated database later.

My Company Ltd Register of documents			
MyCo-CC-DNxxxx.y			
DN	Title	Author	
0001	Company information	A. Person	
0002			
0003			

Figure 4.3. Company register of documents.

Product or service name

Your company name is important, but equally you may be creating a distinct product or service that also merits a name.

Be careful about this, however. Every name you create brings with it sizeable overheads such as the need to generate, promote and maintain a brand. Therefore, if you have a company name, a product name and a service name such as My Company Ltd, SuperWidget and SuperService, you will almost certainly want to consider trademarks, domain names, logos, and so forth for *each* of them. You will also want to make sure you do not fall foul of anyone else's name just as you did with the original company name.

All the same rules apply with a product or service name. Is it memorable, easy to spell, available to use, and so forth? How does it relate in other countries and languages. Even English-speaking countries like the US may not get it as they have different spellings, words and phrases for the same thing?

For highly recommended simplicity, one favoured option is to name the product or service the same as the company. Facebook, for example is Facebook Inc. and the service it offers is Facebook. It started out as The Facebook and famously dropped the definitive article. No confusion, no need to spend money on multiple brands, and the company has a singular focus that employees, shareholders and customers the world over understand.

Google is similar, although it has now created a mother company called Alphabet to hold its numerous speculative ventures. However, even where multiple services exist, they tend to be Google this and Google that (like Google Mail, Google Maps, Google Calendar and so on). Again, this is an efficient and simple approach to branding multiple products and/or services.

Some company brands involve using product numbers and letters. Over time these may be trademarked or inextricably linked to the company, but at the outset they do not need too much additional protection. For example, car manufacturers often produce numbered products. BMW for example produces the 3 series, 5 series, X series and so on. Audi produces the A3, A4, A5, etc. Tesla produces the Model S and Model X.

Apple on the other hand has the iPod, iPhone and iPad to name but a few, so here there are numerous product names in addition to the company name. These are, of course, strong brands, but they took a lot of success and money to become globally recognised.

Exit warrant

Make sure you are not knowingly using a company, product or service name that someone is using elsewhere. Firstly, you will be spending a lot of time and energy building the brand, and secondly, this will become a valuable part of your business that investors will be drawn to and acquirers will like to own. Changing your brand in the future because of a cease-and-desist letter should not be part of the business plan.

If you decide on a product or service name, add this to your company information document as well, writing it down in the way it should be written (for example with upper and lower cases, hyphenation, and so forth). Once again this is an important step because future members of staff will otherwise get this wrong. When Singular ID was acquired, our new owners decided to rebrand the principal product to non-clonable ID, but the marketing collateral soon contained nonclonableID, nonClonableID (TM), NCID, nonclonableID, Non-clonableID, nciD and nCID.

Try to keep names simple and unambiguous so that there is a reduced likelihood of confusion in the future, both internally to your company, but also amongst customers in your marketplace.

Take-away and to-do list:

- Check and check again that your proposed company name is not already in use and that it is not too similar to someone else's identity or trademark.

- A company short code with associated country identifier may seem a little over the top at this stage but will become really useful moving forward.

☐ Company name identified.

☐ First product or service name (if you really must).

☐ Domain name identified.

☐ Short-form company code with territory created, eg, MyCo-CC.

☐ First assets relabeled and asset register modified to reflect this scalable system.

☐ First documents reclassified to reflect the MyCo-CC-DNxxxx.1 convention.

☐ Document register created.

5.

BEST-LAID BUSINESS PLANS

First-cut business plan

We are already at Chapter 5 and we have not even completed our business plan yet. Business plans are a divisive issue. The entrepreneur has it hard-wired in his or her head, has a gut feeling it will all work wonderfully and has not the time to write it all down anyway. Meanwhile, the bank manager or investor will not make another move until they have read and analyzed the business plan to death.

I once had a potential investor come back to me specifically singling out and querying cell 22F in my Excel spreadsheet of financials accompanying my business plan. This was not a headline figure like an annual total, but just a monthly expenditure projection amongst many. That investor later turned down the opportunity to invest, and missed out on a many-times return just two years later. Cell 22F was only an educated guess, but it clearly bothered the investor, and so it is well worth substantiating guesses with some assumptions to avoid confusion; jobsworth or otherwise.

There has to be some middle ground. The business plan is important if you need to raise money, but it should also be important because of the time and energy investment you yourself are about to make. Treat it as a sanity check and a way to flesh out more detail around your business idea. Use it as a live document that will be reviewed and updated by you and your management team regularly in the future. In this way, you will have a way of looking back at what you thought a few months or years ago, letting you see what you got right and what you got wrong. It will become a really useful record that will help you plan your business with more accuracy after each iteration.

If there are co-founders or other members of the management team already in place, make the exercise of writing the business plan a shared duty and a collaborative affair. This will ensure everyone buys into the strategy, but also it will provide more ideas, different points of view, and likely lead to fewer mistakes.

The structure of the business plan is also important. This is partly governed by your audience; investors will indeed require a fair amount of financial detail both past and future. But equally, you will be updating and reviewing the document going forward, so making it well organized and succinct will help you immensely.

The business plan should adopt the document and version number convention described previously, so very likely (unless you have been busy between pages of this book) this will be the first version of the second controlled document which can therefore be labelled MyCo-CC-DN0002.1

Business plan structure

Start with an executive summary first, but come back to compose the body of this chapter when you have written the rest. The key sections of the business plan should be something along the lines of:

Introduction
What your business is all about and why; where is the demand for your product or service, why is it needed, and why is the timing right? Any overall achievements so far (date of incorporation if you have already done this, website, and so forth). This is also your chance to include your vision, mission and core values. I know they are probably a little grating, but you will get extra marks for putting them in your business plan, and if they are not relevant now is the time to change them.

Market
Describe what the opportunity size is, what your price points are,

and what your differentiators are that will make you win customers, including the value proposition. What do you need to do to address the market now and going forward? Any market research or references to date; for example, letters of intent, conditional orders etc.

Competition

Cover who your key competitors are, where they are based, what their approach is, what their strengths are and what you are doing or going to do differently. Answer a key question for the reader: are any competitors' potential partners or suitors for your exit in the future?

Product, service, technology

Discuss what exactly it is that you are going to develop (if applicable) and sell. Do you have patent protection or other intellectual property that creates value? What is the status of your offering, has it been prototyped, tested and sold already? Describe what there is still to do. Technology businesses tend to fall into the trap of going overboard in this section. Yes, a clear description of your novel technology is important, but it should not be out of proportion with all the other chapters.

Customers

If you have some already, elaborate on their motivation to buy from you and how you have delivered. If you have yet to make a sale, use this section to outline the prospective customers you have met with, demonstrated your product or service to, and the feedback that you have obtained. Then use this chapter to provide some customer acquisition targets (what sector, what names, how many) and the associated sales targets (financial value, capacity for repeat custom, level of after sales support needed).

Team

Your own background; any other key team members' background; and who you are looking to recruit in the future. Project the size of team you anticipate in future years and how it will be structured;

for example, more technical people, more sales, overseas agents etc. Include a current and future organization chart, and include brief biographies of the board of directors and, where applicable, the board of advisors.

Finances

Having set out all the details above, now is the time to put numbers to it all. Look at the costs of all the staff and development overheads over time, and look at the build costs and selling price of your products or services. This can be usefully broken down into a few key sections. Firstly, project the sales revenue including costs and hence gross income over time. Are these realistic and achievable? Then look at the overheads. Create a detailed monthly projection for a year and add three subsequent ones. Until you start, do not put in real dates, but rather say M1 for month 1 etc. If you need investment, this often takes longer than you expect, and usually your receipt of funding is the trigger from which you start the financials.

You will probably be doing this number-crunching in a spreadsheet like Microsoft Excel. This spreadsheet is an important document in its own right, even if you copy and paste the figures into your business plan document. As such, these financial projections should be saved using the controlled document system as, for example, MyCo-CC-DN0003.1. The actual figures may not be right, but they should contain key assumptions and good estimates. You can reference MyCo-CC-DN0003.1 as the source of the numbers in the business plan. Similarly, you can reference the mission and vision to MyCo-CC-DN0001.1.

Almost without realizing it you are creating a chain of referenced controlled documents of which an International Standards Organization (ISO) consultant would be proud.

Within your financial projections and business plan, make some assumptions and stress test your basic projection. Look at the effect of more or fewer sales, and indeed the effect of sales coming in later. Ideally you can then produce a bad (worst) case scenario, an ideal case scenario, and a good (best) case scenario with clear associated assumptions for each. Investors really like this approach, and you will find this analysis useful in the future because you can look back and see if any of the assumptions were correct and whether you were too bullish or too bearish.

Of course, if you already have a trading history or money has been spent elsewhere (such as in a university) then add this historical information in too. Investors like to see a track record, and it can be sobering for the entrepreneur to see on paper what has already been spent (or not generated pre-sales).

Next steps and exit

Here is your final section. It is where investors will be drawn and you should outline the end goal you have in mind. Explain how you will develop your business for a trade sale or stock-market listing within a specified timeframe and at a likely valuation. You can use recent examples of companies in your market sector being sold or listing on a stock market to justify your arguments. This is also where you set out your investment needs and summarize the key steps going forward.

Once you have written your first draft, ensure that the title, author(s), and contact details are included on the cover page. Assuming you have written it all yourself and not copied large chunks from the internet, add a copyright statement to the front page as well, including the © symbol, the year and your company. This will show that the copyright is clearly assigned to your business giving you some protection over people just copying your text (not your business idea) and also giving the reader some comfort that the company has the rights to the plan, rather than you, the founder.

As illustrated in Figure 5.1, you should also add a header throughout that states 'confidential information', and a footer referring to MyCo-CC-DN0002.1, as well as the author, date and page number. Whilst you are still working on the draft, write 'issued by: pending'. Only when the document is ready to send to someone will it be issued, then any further amendments will be captured in a subsequent version such as 2.2. This system of document control will help you keep track of what the latest version of the business plan is and what particular version (and, therefore, what content) went to a particular recipient.

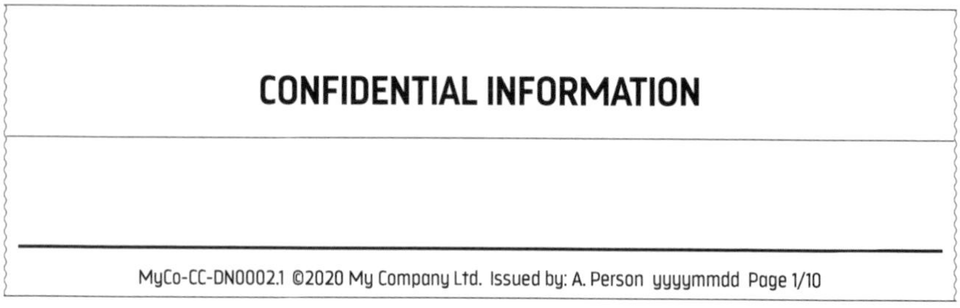

MyCo-CC-DN0002.1 ©2020 My Company Ltd. Issued by: A. Person yyyymmdd Page 1/10

Figure 5.1. Example header and footer for controlled documents such as the business plan.

Optimize your plan

As you work through some of the further chapters of this book, you will be able to hone your business plan. Similarly, whilst you continue to operate your business, you can add and remove information to keep the business plan current.

Try to keep the business plan realistic, succinct and useful to you. If you are kidding yourself, you might as well not bother. Equally, if it becomes a long, drawn-out document that is difficult to navigate and full of waffle, you are unlikely to use and update it, never mind impress a potential investor.

Diagrams, figures and photographs are useful not only to window dress the document but also to explain some of the concepts or summarize some of the content for the less well-versed investor. Bank managers, business angels and venture capitalists see lots of business plans, so if yours looks professional and accessible, it will probably be much better received.

Finally, use references and appendices to substantiate your claims or underpin your data. This is useful for you to refer back to later, helping you to remember where that vital market data or quotation came from. It also allows you to elaborate on, for example, some sales analysis, product development data or intellectual property without ruining the flow of the main text. Structured well, you will be able to update things in future versions without having to edit the narrative too much either.

Understand your audience

Remember again who the audience is for your business plan. Primarily it is you and your co-directors or senior management team, so make it a working document. But also remember it is for your potential financiers who will hopefully treat it as confidential information, but are notoriously difficult to get to sign a non-disclosure agreement to do so. As such, do not give away trade secrets or overly sensitive customer or sales data in the first instance. You can allude to this and provide some details separately later as trust is gained and momentum builds towards a deal.

Many investors you court will walk away, and some will have your competitors in their portfolio. Despite what they will almost certainly say about internal firewalls being in place, information will leak and there is probably not a great deal you can do about it when you are small, poor and vulnerable. Therefore, do be careful what you tell other organizations in your business plan; a sanitized or redacted version for initial enquiries can therefore be useful. If you do this, consider referring to it as MyCo-CC-DN0002.1a. The 'a' in this case helps to manage subsets of a master document. This means you know that the version is modified from 2.1 helping you to go back to the parent version more quickly and to log that this version was not derived from a later iteration such as 2.2 for example.

Finally, business plans are documents about seeking investment from sophisticated investors, they are not suitable for the general public. You need to add one more paragraph of text to the cover page to explain that this is not a public offering and that investments like the one you describe carry substantial risk. If you look around on the internet, you will find plenty of boilerplate text along these lines that you may like to use, subject to your own verification of its suitability.

Exit warrant

Your business plan will form a key part of any investment or acquisition, and you will be asked to confirm that it is a true and accurate representation of the business as it currently stands and is planned to move forward. Do not hide things or make misrepresentations in this document or any associated spreadsheets. Equally, do not guarantee things that you have little or no control over: ensure projections are stated as such. Your business plan's targets are likely to be the milestones you will be measured against to release more funds or keep your job, so make sure you are happy with them as written.

Other analysis useful for planning

The way I have described the business plan above is as a traditional written document. There are, of course, other sections and analyses you could add. For example, you may want to provide a SWOT analysis of your strengths, weaknesses, opportunities and threats. This can also be useful to monitor over time, as hopefully you will build on your strengths, tackle your weaknesses, seize your opportunities and see off the threats. By keeping an updated view of your SWOT, you will certainly develop your business in the right direction.

Management consultants have a whole arsenal of business planning and strategic planning tools up their sleeve, but all they really do is help you to analyze aspects of the business and its operations to augment your business plan. Adding them to your plan needs to bring you benefit, but they can also show a potential investor that you have thought about the business from various angles and are professional in your management approach.

Value chain analysis
Value chain analysis can be useful to understand the stakeholders in your supply chain through to your customers and finally the end

customers. An understanding of how components of your product or service come together and are sold on is important because you will be able to see if you are reliant on a few key suppliers and also if you have a strong enough place in the supply chain so as not to be cut out of it. You may also see opportunities for vertical integration in which you could add activities up and down the supply chain yourself, thus growing your business and becoming less reliant on others. Tetrapak is a good example of a vertically integrated business, owning the forests that provide the trees that go to their pulping facilities that produce their packaging that go in their machines that their customers lease.

But note that this kind of analysis is dynamic, so putting it in your business plan is one thing, but coming back to it and keeping it assessed and updated is really the crucial task.

Roadmap
Project managers like to use flow charts or, better still Gantt charts, to plan and execute complicated tasks. These are often too detailed for a top-level business plan unless the project described is of the business itself. Such a chart is then often termed a business or operational roadmap. As shown in Figure 5.2, a roadmap tells you when you plan to do something, why you want to do it, what you will actually need to do, and how you will achieve it.

The roadmap succinctly shows the business drivers: what you as a business want to achieve over time, sometimes termed your internal drivers; the market drivers (key external trends that are outside of your direct control in the real world); the planned evolution of your products and services (in effect your catalogue); and the technology capability you will need to develop and deliver new products and/or services in a timely manner. The roadmap can also capture your resource plan such as changes in staffing and utilizing collaborating partners.

Including a roadmap in your company's business plan can be a really helpful exercise, because it is a very visual way to depict how your business will develop. It is often best constructed as part of a team exercise involving your key decision-makers, but for the start-up this is likely to be the founders or directors. There are detailed methodologies available for running workshops and building roadmaps, and it is something I have done with numerous companies and organizations in the UK, Singapore, Saudi Arabia and Taiwan.

Invaluable capex

A set of coloured sticky notes, marker pens and A2 flip chart paper is a worthwhile investment for team workshops and brainstorming. You can jot key points onto the notes, coloured for different themes, and create your own roadmap. Or you can just use them to create plenty of ideas to distil into your business plan. £10 outlay

---

Using sticky notes and jotting down ideas will probably get you there in the start-up phase so that you have something like that shown in Figure 5.3. The key point is to look for the linkages over time as illustrated with the dotted line. In summary, resources need to be in place to develop the technology that feeds into a product or service offering. These in turn should be on time to meet both a business milestone and a market need.

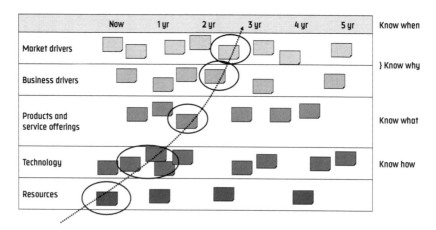

Figure 5.2. A strategic business roadmap compiled by using key points on sticky notes.

Just as the financial projections were given a controlled document number, so too should the roadmap, as it is likely to have been compiled in a separate document and brought into the overall business plan. Hence, the document containing the roadmap could be designated MyCo-CC-DN0004.1, creating a reference for the business plan and other documents or presentations that make use of it.

Business Model Canvas
A pictorial tool to help describe a business model; the actual nuts and bolts of creating revenue in your company. A business model is a little different to a financial projection or a business plan because it is the formula, if you like, that enables the financial projections to be calculated and the business plan to be elaborated. Top-level business models can include charges for product sales, billing hourly for consultancy time, and charging annually for a per user (per seat) software license.

Clearly, these are important considerations for your business and you should have a clear business model (or models) and be prepared to test and change them. Having an agile business that can adapt business models to address the market pull will make growth easier. It will also impress investors or potential acquirers and demonstrate that the business has tested its market over time and evolved to try to maximize sales revenue.

The Business Model Canvas helps you understand the value chain, the cost model, the sales potential and the interdependent factors that control these variables.

Monitor and update your plan

As you run your business and execute your business plan, you will be able to look back over it and see what was right and what was wrong. More sophisticated businesses will try to monitor key performance indicators (KPIs) like monthly sales, warehouse stock levels, delivery times and customer complaints, linking them to certain strategies like improving a sales process or introducing parts of an enterprise resource planning system. This leads to other management tools like the balanced scorecard.

By now your controlled document register is also starting to fill up. It should look something like that below in Figure 5.3. Note that the register does not try to capture the version numbers, just the document number and what it relates to. Anyone in the company who refers to the register can see that the document with the title exists and who wrote it.

My Company Ltd Register of documents		
MyCo-CC-DNxxxx.y		
DN	**Title**	**Author**
0001	Company information	A. Person
0002	Business plan	A. Person
0003	Financials projections	A. Person
0004	Business roadmap	A. Person

Figure 5.3. The growing content of the document register.

Take-away and to-do list

- Write your business plan primarily for yourself and your co-founders or management team.

- Then use it for potential investors, but be wary of how much information you give away whilst always being truthful with what is stated and clear with what is projected.

- Start to record important documents and spreadsheets using a document-number and version-number system for traceability and to help everyone in the company to refer to the most up-to-date one.

☐ First business plan drafted.

☐ Financials spreadsheet.

☐ Documents filed and referenced using the system MyCo-CC-DN0000x.y.

6.

COMPANY SHARES AND SHARES ALIKE

A stake in your company

You can start a business without creating a company, and you can get lots of up-to-date advice on whether it is better to be a sole trader, a limited liability partnership, a co-operative, a community interest company, or a private limited company. You need to look at this from the cost of running the type of company you chose, the way you will be paid (salary vs dividends), and whether you plan to seek further investment in the future.

However, I am going to focus on the limited company, because this is the likely legal entity for the kind of growth business that most people end up developing on the entrepreneurial journey towards venture capital investment, trade sale or listing.

The limited company is comprised of shares; basically slices or stakes of a business with different ownership. It is not difficult to fill out a few forms and issue shares as part of the incorporation process of a company, on-line through Companies House in the UK for example, but I have found a few things are useful to know in advance.

Many people just create a company of one share (for example, if it is just themselves starting out) or two shares (for example, if they want to include their spouse or co-founding business partner) or a few shares each for good measure if a small group of two or three are starting out.

That is all fine, but it can make things a little more difficult later on. Although the concept of par value (the nominal or face value of a share) is somewhat arbitrary at the start, it is worth considering what it might mean to you later. Much of this is psychological, but never-the-less important if you are to succeed in the game you are about to play.

If you are creating a lifestyle business for just yourself, or indeed you and your life partner, then it might be okay to issue just a few shares each. However, even in this situation I would suggest that you issue of the order of 1,000 shares each and set the par value as either 1p, 10p or £1 per share depending in your appetite. So, if you and your business partner each own 50% with 1,000 shares each valued at £1 per share, you each need to pay in £1000 of capital.

Invaluable capex

Put some skin in the game and purchase a small but meaningful number of shares in your own company to provide initial working capital and a seminal share price. Work hard and with a bit of luck you will get it all back many thousands of times over. Personal outlay: £1000 or more.

This gives the company some valuable equity to work with, shows a share structure that suggests depth, and gives you a little flexibility to play with in the future should someone else come on board. Do note that this share capital is locked into the company, so do not invest £1000 each if you are going to need the money back before an exit. Rather, set the par value lower and loan the company additional capital so it can be paid back sooner.

Structuring for subsequent investment

If you look at the case of a high-tech start-up that might need angel and then venture capital (VC) investment the situation might develop in the following way.

If you are one of two founders, then in this example let us consider you incorporate the company with 10,000 shares each at £1 per share so that you each invest £10,000. This act demonstrates to a future investor that you have courage in your convictions; it is after all a fair amount of money for an individual to stump up and risk. The company then has a working capital of £20,000 to get going, and its initial share price is a reasonably straight forward £1. Of course, you could start with a different par value or different number of shares and invest more or less at this point as you see fit. Your capitalization table is an important working document, and so you can create a spreadsheet MyCo-CC-DN0005.1 to keep track of it. Moreover, once compiled, you will probably want to add it as an appendix to your business plan. By making reference to the document number, you will know which version you are using. Table 6.1 shows the effects of various stages of investment.

How rounds of investment may then play out

Next, if you have some intellectual property that you can in-license (as might be the case if you are a university spin-off), or you set to work on the business and secure a first sale, you can start to argue the company's value is now a little higher. The taxman will generally look at this objectively (like how much money you have in the bank and the value of your tangible assets: ie, the 'real' paper value of the company). But you can start to be more optimistic in terms of pitching to an investor (or more likely at this stage friends and family). For example, you can say that now you have designed a logo, set up a website, started to draft a patent application, and maybe secured a contract for a future sale; the share price is now £2 per share. Of course, this is up for negotiation, but let us assume this is the value settled on by all concerned. This is a 100% growth rate reflecting the value of your (possibly unpaid) effort over a period of time and the creation of some important intellectual property. Friends and family can now buy into the company at this increased share price and because you have already issued 20,000 shares, you are in a position to issue more at the new value without needing to split any of the existing shares and creating more unnecessary complication. For example, your friend might now invest

£5000 for 2500 shares. This sets the right tone for growth as the share price is going up and the number of shares issued is commensurate. As founders you have not made any further investment, so your stake is diluted (you each own proportionately less of the company). You could invest at the same share price, although if you did, you would have to ask yourself why you were also bringing in friends and family at this stage and not just topping up the investment (or making a loan) yourselves without adding the complication of other shareholders to the mix.

A total of 22,500 shares have now been issued and your friend investor owns 2500 of them which is just over 10% of the company. Take a look at Table 6.1 to see this investment round summarized.

Now you continue to add value that will attract an angel investor; for example, you finish drafting your patent application or design right and file it at the Intellectual Property Office. You also build a prototype and firm up the sales contract off the back of it for which you need some additional capital to see it all through. The business is now showing significantly more potential and after some negotiation you obtain £20,000 investment from an angel investor at £5 per share. This is 4000 shares, so the total issued share capital of the company is now 26,500 shares, and the existing shareholders have been diluted a little further. As the two founders, you own 20,000 of the company's 26,500 shares between you, which is still over 75% (so you remain in control, as indeed founders should at this stage). The angel has 4000 of the 26,500 shares, which is a healthy 15% stake for a relatively large and risky investment at this stage. After putting in as much cash as the founders did originally at a considerably higher price, but you have reduced the risk by demonstrating success and working hard to add value. This story is certainly compelling if you have not been drawing (much of) a salary up until this stage.

You will also note that the post-money valuation of the company is going up too. This is calculated from the total number of issued shares multiplied by the last share price paid. It is only a paper value at the moment, and could go down quite easily if you are compelled to take money at a lower price in the future, but this post-money valuation is a key parameter to keep an eye on.

After this angel round closes, the company makes its first product delivery and obtains real revenue against its first proper sale. This leads to a repeat customer and perhaps a new customer. You have continued to work for low pay, but money is now running low due to scaling-up operations putting yet more demands on your cash flow. A further investor may now be needed, for example a seed capital investor (early stage venture capital). Now you could be arguing you share price is £20 per share and seeking £140,000 capital. This would be 7000 new shares, so the capitalization table grows further as shown in Table 6.1.

Of course, this is an idealistic scenerio and nothing goes quite this smoothly in reality. But you can see by way of example that the share price has been steadily rising and the number of investors growing as the risks reduce and the need for capital grows. The level of control is spreading between different parties, but still the driving force (the founders) remain interested, motivated, and keen to succeed. In this example, the founders still own 60% of the company and so have retained a controlling stake.

Most importantly, because of the way the initial shares were issued when the company was founded, you have also been able to issue new share capital easily without complicated re-structuring and whilst maintaining a coherent and compelling story. It is not essential, but it gives you the edge and clarity as you seek investment and defend your progress.

Investment round	Shareholder	Number of shares	Price per share	This investment	Investment to date	Post money valuation	Ownership
0: incorporation	Founder 1	10,000	£1.00	£10,000	£10,000	£10,000	50%
	Founder 2	10,000	£1.00	£10,000	£10,000	£10,000	50%
	Total	20,000	£1.00	£20,000	£20,000	£20,000	100%
1: friends and family	Founder 1	10,000	£2.00	-	£10,000	£20,000	44.5%
	Founder 2	10,000	£2.00	-	£10,000	£20,000	44.5%
	Friend 1	2,500	£2.00	£5,000	£5,000	£5,000	11%
	Total	22,500	£2.00	£5,000	£25,000	£45,000	100%
2: angel investor	Founder 1	10,000	£5.00	-	£10,000	£50,000	38%
	Founder 2	10,000	£5.00	-	£10,000	£50,000	38%
	Friend 1	2,500	£5.00	-	£5,000	£12,500	9%
	Angel 1	4,000	£5.00	£20,000	£20,000	£20,000	15%
	Total	26,500	£5.00	£20,000	£45,000	£132,500	100%
3: early venture capital	Founder 1	10,000	£20.00	-	£10,000	£200,000	30%
	Founder 2	10,000	£20.00	-	£10,000	£200,000	30%
	Friend 1	2,500	£20.00	-	£5,000	£50,000	7%
	Angel 1	4,000	£20.00	-	£20,000	£80,000	12%
	VC 1	7,000	£20.00	£140,000	£140,000	£140,000	21%
	Total	33,500	£20.00	£140,000	£185,000	£670,000	100%

Table 6.1. The capitalization table up to and including the first round of venture capital investment.

Testing scenarios with the capitalization table

Moreover, you can vary the numbers in the spreadsheet to project how things could play out differently. What is the impact of taking more investment at a given share price or not getting as high a share price as perhaps hoped? The message here is that just as you would create a budget or sales forecast, you should also produce a capitalization table forecast. At each juncture, you can review it against previous projections and see if you made sensible assumptions and set realistic targets. You will also see how your company is growing in value and the impact of taking different levels of investment at future points in time.

Of course, you cannot get hung up on all of this. Forecasts are forecasts, and the reality at a particular time when you take or leave investment will present itself with a specific set of issues and considerations. As everyone keeps warning you, the value of investments can go up or down and you may not get any or all of your original money back.

It is also worth understanding the drivers for the investors and how much control they will expect. Television programmes like Dragons' Den and The Apprentice have distorted the market a little, because they make the argument that having a celebrity investor brings untold connections and marketing clout. This may be true, and certainly the television show itself can be invaluable marketing. However, having an angel investor at this early stage taking a large slice of your business can be counterproductive, because in my view where multiple rounds of investment are going to be sought, there is a narrow band in which to work that keeps the founders motivated and does not create reporting or compliance issues for the corporate or venture capital investor.

For example, a venture capitalist is not usually going to take more than 50% of your business because then you have become a subsidiary. Secondly, 20% is another interesting threshold because of the corporate influence and reporting requirements with respect to equity accounting legislation and the onus of acts such as Sarbanes Oxley in the US. In the example above, the early-stage venture capitalist ended up with 21% of the company. In reality, they may actually wish to be

19% (so knowing this, you can pitch the share price accordingly). Note that venture capitalists also try to gain more influence by teaming up, so for example, two each having 19% will have 38% between them, and often they share the same goals so work together to drive shareholder decisions.

Exit warrant

Keep you capitalization table up to date and include all the share transactions on it. Do not promise someone shares for a service in lieu of a cash payment and then omit them from the table, as these agreements will have a real impact on your attractiveness to investors. You will also have to vouch that the capitalization table is accurate and you will be responsible to settle with anyone that comes out of the woodwork with a claim at a later date. This would be a good example of an unacceptable skeleton in the closet: if they have shares they should be listed in the capitalization table as well.

Other considerations about shares

What we have not considered here are all the other provisions that investors might put in place, particularly venture capitalists who are more sophisticated. These provisions can include tag-along, drag-along, pre-emption and anti-dilution rights, any of which can have a significant impact on your capitalization table after each funding round.

Try not to over-complicate other related matters too early on either. Investors will almost certainly ask for preference shares in later years (shares with different rights attached to them, mainly to mitigate their risk and enhance their upside), but to begin with you would be wise to issue ordinary shares at the outset for the founders, and possibly preference A shares when 'real' third-party money is being invested by angels or venture capitalists.

Sometimes it is beneficial to have two classes of ordinary shares, say for a husband-and-wife partnership, as that way different levels of dividends can be paid to each to more effectively tax plan or to reflect levels of effort at different stages of the business. To me, this is a lifestyle business consideration.

Share splitting is where the pool is enlarged by splitting everyone's shares. The result can give a higher level of precision (or resolution) when issuing new shares, although it is better to start out with a larger pool in the first place. When Peter and I started Singular ID, we were not altogether familiar with these concepts, so we created a company with two shares, one each with a par value of one Singapore dollar. Hence the company had two dollars of paid-up capital and we owned half of it each. We then realized that taking on our first angel investor, and injecting some more working capital ourselves was instantly problematic. Returning to our accountant, we explained the situation. Oddly enough, this also seemed news to him too; a case of the blind leading the blind. But, despite his reservations as to the necessity, we went on to split the shares into thousands and it all worked out in the end.

Eventually, you might find that you still reach a limit even having issued plenty of shares, so at that point you can always go ahead and split them. You can, for example, say that the existing 53,000 shares of par value £1, but current share price £10 are to be split into ten, so there will be 530,000 shares issued with a new par value of 10p, share price £1. You can see that this can get messy if the par value has already been set at 1p, as then you start to split pennies. This is okay, but adds unnecessary confusion to the situation.

I am often asked what paid-up capital really means and what value does it actually have. If you create a company of just two shares with a par value of £1 each, issue them and receive this value into the company to make them 'paid up', then your balance sheet has £2 paid-up capital. This is fine, but does not send a message of having made much of an investment or commitment to the company. The company is effectively guaranteed by its share capital, so the value of this notional guarantee is not very high. If someone has invested a few thousand pounds or dollars, it sounds more credible. This can also give more comfort to suppliers and collaborators, as they will consider the company to have more financial gravitas. Of course, the paid-up share capital can be spent, so it is not really there as a perpetual guarantee. Also, if something does go wrong, that money (or what is left of it) can be lost to the shareholders through the liquidation process as they are generally last in line to receive any of the funds.

Investor psychology

It is also worth highlighting that the notion of par value and the actual cost of an individual share is psychological. In the case of Singular ID, as founders, we once had a meeting with an incubation partner who was convinced that shares costing $10 to $100 were highly unusual and too expensive, so should be split to be of the order of $1 again. Today you just have to look at the likes of Apple and Google to know that this is nonsense, because as I write, Apple shares are over $100 a piece, and Google's are over $800. The point is that it is simply psychological; it all boils down to the value of the company and the number shares that make up that company. If you create a company with just one share and sell that company for £1m, then that is quite simply the price of the share.

A crowd of shareholders

Having lots of shareholders can be problematic. Firstly, you have a duty to shareholders to maximize value. It demands good governance, as well as communicating to shareholders the progress that is being made. They also need to be given the opportunity to vote about certain matters. So, the fewer you have, the easier they will be to both manage and appease during the early stages of business growth.

Moreover, above a certain threshold of shareholders, a private limited company becomes by definition a public limited company. This limit varies from country to country, and can result in the need for more financial disclosure and add to your board members' workloads.

You must also take care in how you seek investment and offer shares to people. In the UK, you must not offer shares to the general public on your website, for example, as this is considered a public offering and requires certain licenses and procedures to be met. As such, the relatively new process of crowdfunding requires care in its implementation. If, however, you go down the crowdfunding route, much of the previous discussion still applies in that you will be issuing shares to one or more investors and your capitalization table will be adjusted accordingly.

That said, shares can certainly be a good way to motivate and retain key members of staff in a business. These shares are often handled through a share option pool for tax efficiency and to simplify the management process, but they would and should still appear in the capitalization table when in existence.

As your group of shareholders grow, so your shareholders' expectation may diversify. If shareholders expect dividends, then retaining profits in the business to fund future operations could be difficult. Therefore, it is also important for all the shareholders to be aligned with the business plan; is the aim to grow a company rapidly, sell and realize a capital gain, or is the aim to generate profits that are distributed through dividends to provide an income and perhaps have a slow-growth company?

A small slice of something big

You will often hear from investors that owning a small slice of something big is better than owning a large slice of nothing. Although this is undeniably true, they use this argument to persuade the founders to accept a lower valuation so that the investor owns a larger percentage of the company. Their justification is that their involvement will bring untold intangible value through connections and experience so that the business will grow more quickly and be that much more valuable.

A counterargument, should you need one, is the same; if they take a big slice, you as a founder will not feel as motivated and their stake, though larger, will become worthless. It is therefore better for them to have a smaller slice of something that you as founders are motivated to grow.

What of the friend? He still only has 2,500 shares in an issued pool of 33,500, so he only owns about 7% of the company now. But his share value has been, on paper at least, growing: his initial investment of £5000 is now deemed to be worth £50,000 as the share price is now £20 per share. Note that he has not realized this value because he has not sold his shares, and is unlikely to do so for some time for reasons we will discuss later. But the message is clear to all: investors are potentially making money and the trend has been set for a high-growth company with a share structure that has worked without any share splits or other tinkering at the sidelines.

Future investors, as the stakes go up, will become more and more sophisticated. When they start circling they will be pleased to see the trend of increasing value outlined in your capitalization table during their own due diligence. They will be able to see the transactions clearly, they will see it has been a clean well-structured company without complicated shady share transactions on the side, and they will be comforted in the way the company has been managed and grown. As proof, the capitalization table shows that people have been buying in at progressively higher valuations.

It is this kind of approach that makes your company more sellable in the future. After all, your primary aim should be to position your company for a quick, lucrative and smooth exit. Even if it is years in the future, getting things right early on helps immensely.

Take-away and to-do list

- Set a low par value for shares and issue a good number at the outset so that each founder holds thousands of shares. This gives more precision in the future when further shares are issued to investors or staff.

- A share capitalisation table is not only a record of the shares and associated pre-money and post-money valuation of a company at each stage, it can also be used to model future scenarios towards the exit to optimise the pitch and tune the level of investment sought.

☐ Start a share capitalization table for the company and keep it updated.

7.

IN THE BEGINNING, THERE IS INCORPORATION

The first steps in formalizing a company

You might think that Chapter 7 is a little late in the day to be talking about the beginning. Moreover, if you have been following the actions in this book, you probably cannot help but notice that we still have not gone ahead and formed the company yet. This just goes to underline that preparation is everything.

There are a few basics to get right first, as these help all the other things fall into place afterwards. One of the key points at this stage is to keep accurate and retrievable records from the start and try not to mess things up in this crucial initial phase.

The company's constitution

You can create a company using a standard set of documents, but just check that the memorandum and the articles of association are what you expect. These are effectively the company's rule book or constitution. Some of it is cast in company law and cannot be changed, but carefully read through and understand what it says about shares, shareholder votes, shareholder meetings, directors, board meetings and board member votes.

Keep a watch on the various quorums needed for meetings and for votes to count. Do not stipulate you need two directors if it is just you, but also consider how things might play out if you take on new shareholders or if investors become board members. The details can be changed in future, but, if what you have is sensible to begin with, it will require less work and reassure potential investors.

Also check that in this modern age that you can hold meetings and pass resolutions when people are present by telephone or something equivalent like iChat or Skype, and that notices, agendas and meetings can be circulated by email. This will make things a lot simpler as you grow and have stakeholders located away from you head office. Bring the memorandum and articles of association into your document list as, for example, MyCo-CC-DN0006.1.

Shareholders' agreement

Separate to the constitution is a shareholders' agreement. This is a binding agreement between the shareholders beyond the articles of association that outlines the conduct of the shareholders to protect each other's interests. This document can become quite extensive when more sophisticated venture capital investors come on board. At this stage, just consider a few things, especially if you are two or more founders who have got together to embark on the venture:

Firstly, write down something about non-competing as a shareholder; this can include conflicts of interest that must be declared or avoided such as investing in or working for another company in the same sector.

Then consider what happens if one of you wants to (or is forced through unforeseen circumstances) to leave and/or sell their shares. Usually, you will want to prohibit them being sold in full or in part to a third party unless all shareholders are selling, or unless each shareholder has given written permission. This situation can sometimes cause problems as one shareholder may veto a transaction, so another option is to add that when an authentic third-party offer is tabled, the same terms are first offered to the other existing shareholders.

What happens if a founder dies in service? Usually it is worth having an agreement where it is stated the shares can be transferred to their heirs, but perhaps the voting rights are divided amongst the surviving founders so that the company can follow its agreed strategy.

It is more tricky if a founder leaves. In this case, they will no longer be contributing to the company and yet they have their initial stake. Here you could have an agreement that a proportion of shares (such as half) will be cancelled at the end of each subsequent year before an exit. This will diminish their stake whilst the other founders are continuing to work. To avoid conflicts, such as prolonging the completion of a deal to after an impending cancellation date, you could build in that a number of shares are in effect cancelled each day during the year to bring about the overall depletion by half each year.

The key here is that the devil is in the detail and you cannot anticipate every 'blue moon' event. But there are some key things that plague start-up success, and they include founders falling out, changes of circumstances in the team, and new investments being needed.

If you can anticipate a few of these eventualities at the outset and build in some mechanisms to cope with them, then you will save the company and the founders individually a lot on hefty legal bills and distracting litigation.

Three, two, one, incorporate

Once you are settled on a company name, have a business plan more than just in mind, and some understanding of the way share structures might play out, you really are ready to incorporate. You now need to get ready to push the button on a number of other things almost simultaneously.

These next actions will involve:

- registering the domain name (do this first as then you can use your new company email address for the rest of the process);
- registering at Companies House or an equivalent if you are not in the UK;
- setting up a bank account;
- appointing an accountant;

- letting HMRC or an equivalent tax authority know you have started trading;

- and registering your payroll, VAT, corporation tax and so forth, depending on the local rules of the country in which you are incorporating.

You may also need other permits for your line of work (for example, if you plan to operate in the financial services or insurance sector, offer healthcare products or services, and so on).

If you are joining us in this discussion having already incorporated a company and indeed been running for a while, you can still go back and check you have got all these things in place and filed correctly. This is not an exhaustive list, and requirements do change. For example, in the UK new employer pension schemes are being introduced that will mean that company founders will soon have to arrange a company pension scheme from a supplier as part of the start-up phase. If you are going to handle personal information (which most companies do) you may also need to register with the Information Commissioners Office or equivalent.

Keeping files organized

This incorporation stage creates a fair amount of important paperwork that you will need to come back to later. It will form a key part of your company file when it comes to future due diligence by an investor or a potential acquirer.

The way I handle this is to procure and label some good old-fashioned lever arch files, because regardless of how much you want to be fully electronic, you will receive paper at this point, and it would be worth keeping a hard copy even if you do scan and store it electronically as well.

Invaluable capex

Not really capital expenditure, but this is where some stationery purchases comes in useful. Spend some money on lever arch files, dividers and a share-record book. In terms of capital expenditure, it would be well worth buying a lockable company cupboard or filing cabinet in which to store the files securely. Remember to add an asset label to this item using the MyCo-CC-AN00xx format. Stationery outlay: £20. Furniture: £60.

Once you create the company and have issued the shares, you will need the supporting documentation to be filed. A low-cost company book is a worthwhile investment at this stage, as it provides a hard-copy record of your directors, shareholders and other officers (like the generally non-obligatory company secretary). It also provides share certificates with counterfoils to record their issuance. There are also new rules in the UK that state you must keep a list of controlling or influential entities of a business (usually these are shareholders with more than 20% of the voting rights of the company and directors, but the list needs to be correct, so with corporate shareholders you may need to seek specialist advice).

I always scan copies of issued shares, so there is a centralized company record. Making sure the share register is complete and accurate is important because a future investor or acquirer wants to know the full extent of the issued shares and the ownership. Your capitalization table should also reflect these shareholdings, so you can add some further annotations relating to the investment date, certificate numbers and certificate issue dates.

During this crucial phase of incorporating the company, you will have more things to add to the company information document including company registration number, incorporation date, VAT registration number, payroll (PAYE) registration number, and domain name(s). There will also be a growing list of other controlled documents including the capitalization table, memorandum, articles of association and shareholders' agreement.

As a result of these transactions, you will be receiving both hard and electronic copies of important records from different organizations. This is the time to create a lever-arch file labelled 'MyCo BRD' to indicate it is a file of printed records for your company's board of directors.

The hard-copy file can be split later to pass to departments that may perform these functions, but ultimately these are key initial records that the managing director (or CEO) needs to keep safe and refer to. For example, the finance department will manage taxation in the future, but the sensitive information at the start is for the eyes of the board only.

Over the years I have found several sections to be useful:

'General correspondence' can be filed first which is just the miscellaneous letters and paperwork that you receive that fall outside of the main headings.

'Signed agreements' is a general section for executed documents such as memoranda of understanding, non-disclosure agreements, project agreements, and so forth. If your business is likely to generate lots of a certain kind of these, you can of course file them in categories.

'Bank account' is for all your company banking details, usually just a business current account at the outset, but could also include other banking facilities such as corporate credit cards and deposit account.

'Grants and state aid' is a useful section as you start to receive letters summarizing any funds or value received to which you can refer quickly for new applications. This is because there are currently limits to the amount of state aid you can receive in a rolling three-year period, certainly in the EU and possibly elsewhere in the world.

'Compliance' is quite broad, but includes any insurance (for example, employer's liability insurance), registration details with, for example, the Information Commissioner, and any registrations for health and safety.

'Board and shareholder' section will hold original signed minutes and resolutions. Wherever possible, things are often best kept in digital and scanned format, but where original signed documents are generated in the course of running board meetings and shareholder meetings, this is the place to file them.

Finally, there are two sections relating to 'tax authority' correspondence (HMRC in the UK) and 'company registration authority' correspondence (Companies House in the UK). Here you can file your tax details, VAT certificate and original company incorporation certificate.

Exit warrant

This is where you will need to prove that your company was properly incorporated and all the associated documentation, registration information and compliance has been correctly filled out, retained and maintained. Hence, having all the documents filed logically and perhaps scanned electronically will make it a whole lot easier to find and collate during a due diligence exercise.

Staff records

It is also worth creating a separate hard-copy file for human resources (HR) that will relate to confidential staff details, pension and payroll. The first section can contain the correspondence received from the tax authority (HMRC in the UK) relating to payroll, such as payroll number, notifications and so forth. Then I find it useful to have a section for each member of staff and to keep hard copies of their job application, curriculum vitae, interview notes, signed contracts, induction forms, appraisal forms, pay slips, holiday record forms etc. Sometimes hard copies are created because they are physically signed by the member of staff. When such an original is created, it is probably worth filing, even if you do create a scanned version for the server and let your member of staff keep a personal record.

HR information is highly confidential, as it includes staff name, address, date of birth, identity information (like National Insurance number and passport number), financial information (like basic salary, bonuses and tax codes), performance reviews, records of disciplinary action where applicable, and potentially health information. As such, these files need to be kept locked in a secure cupboard or filing cabinet that can only be accessed by designated personal from the board and the HR department. Any electronic copies made also need to be kept securely, raising all kinds of cyber security and privacy issues.

Now, however, you should have a company formed with a number of documents and folders (both electronic and physical hardcopies), filed in a retrievable, appropriately secure, and organized manner, so that you can quickly put your hands on them in the future.

Insurance

At this stage, it is also well worth considering insurance. There are lots of different types of insurance (for example, professional indemnity, public liability, directors, cyber, and buildings and contents), which all cover different risks. This book is not the place to explain them, but rather to highlight the importance of having appropriate policies in place and to make a point of reviewing the terms and conditions to check things are still valid and applicable at renewal. For example, your turnover may have exceeded that stated in the insurance schedule; you may be selling a new product; you may be operating in an overseas market; or you may have more employees than stated.

In some territories like the UK, some insurance is mandatory: a company that employs people must have employer liability insurance. The main thing with insurance is to read the small print and only spend money on what you need, but make sure it does indeed cover you for what you need.

When I sought building and contents insurance for our business centre, I was quoted fairly standard policies that did not cover rented units or the possibility of unoccupied areas. To get something suitable meant talking with a knowledgeable insurance broker who then did much of the legwork based on their experience of working in the industry.

Having insurance policies in place is also a good sign for prospective investors and acquirers. Investors will certainly want appropriate insurance to have been purchased to protect their investment, and acquirers will like to see it, because when policies have been continuously at risk, they provide some historical protection as well. For example, if someone is injured by a product you have been selling for a number of years, and the product liability insurance policy was in place when you sold it and has remained in force for the duration, then it is likely your company is still covered. This greatly lowers the risk of an expensive future claim which will give a lot of comfort to a potential acquirer of your business.

Take-away and to-do list

- Company formation and all the associated activity of setting up a bank account, selecting an accountant, taking out insurance and so on creates a lot of important paperwork that you need to get right and also that you need to file in an organized and retrievable way.

☐ Physical lever arch file of board-related documents labelled and filed.

☐ Physical lever arch file of HR documents labelled and filed.

☐ Secure location, such as a cupboard, earmarked for company documents.

8.

ORGANIZATIONAL DEPARTMENTS AND COMPARTMENTS

Staff functions

One of the problems that comes along with company growth is that you inevitably take on new staff with specific functions, and somehow you need to give them access to the right information within the company without giving them a carte-blanche to your entire repository. Think of this as a need-to-know policy.

To help with this issue, it is useful to create some traditional departments in your fledgling company even though you will probably be the initial head and general dog's body of them all.

Although different companies may have a need for different departments, and you can of course be creative with their names and remits, in the end you'll probably be okay settling for the traditional categories based around job function. If you do not like the word department, you could refer to them as groups, teams or sections. I would not call them divisions because that word is already used to refer to subsets of an organization that include many or all of these departmental functions almost like a separate company.

Despite the digital age, a proportion of information will arrive in hard copy or printed form. If you can digitize as much as possible, and rely on pdf records for example, that helps, but some things still need to be filed as a paper copy. To cope with this, it is helpful to create a library of lever arch files in each department that parallels (but definitely not duplicates) an online repository of information.

Humans like to hoard, gathering knowledge for themselves so that they are informed and remain a crucial cog in the organization. However, humans also change jobs and move on, so your goal is to encourage employees to take ownership of responsibilities, but to share information so that other staff who need to know about it can find it and act on it. Therefore, as much as possible, paperwork and 'datawork' (as you could call it) should be filed in common folders and not in individual's desks nor in personal folders. This can be difficult to achieve and police, so in general it is about creating logical and intuitive structures for people to use with less trouble than creating their own. If they can access more information as a result and speed up their own work, they will soon see the value.

At this stage, the digital repositories for the departments can be created as folders on your own computer or perhaps in a virtual data store (the cloud) in something like Google Drive. However, this should be regarded as a temporary situation just to get you started, as there are privacy, cyber security and scalability issues that we will come to later.

Think of the departments firstly in the form of an organization chart. Sketching it out as to how you see your company in a few years' time is helpful. Clearly at the start-up stage such a structure looks a little over the top, but having this in mind is beneficial as you can see what job functions you expect to have. If you are already beyond the start-up phase, you may already have some of these departments populated, and just doing a sanity check on which ones are missing and which ones have overlaps of function can be useful.

Functions that straddle departments

Functional overlap is one of the problems I wrestle with frequently. Clearly there is an overlap between finance and HR, because payroll involves paying people and so finance will need to be aware what HR knows about employee's pay. In an advanced system, you would want shared permissions for this bit of information across the two departments. And there are plenty of other examples like this; the sales team needs access and influence over the branding details managed by marketing. However, the good news is that a little forethought and planning can identify these overlaps and ensure that by and large a system is put in place where control resides with one group and limited need-to-know access lies elsewhere.

A good generic start for the departmental structure is shown below in Figure 8.1

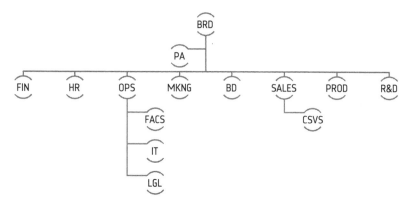

Figure 8.1. Generic corporate structure of departments.

The board of directors

The first, overarching department is of course the board (BRD). Members of the board can have access to all the company information, but will also have some information that only the board should see. These will be board reports, board meeting minutes, some strategic plans and possibly some top-secret or market sensitive agreements. Note that the trusted personal assistant (PA) to the directors may also be permitted to see the board's confidential information because the company is unlikely to function on a day-to-day basis without this. But this access may be further limited as the PA may not be privy to everything.

Finance

The next department or team to consider is finance (FIN). You can think of this department of next importance after the board because money management is what allows the rest of the company to exist. The functions of this department will include bookkeeping, accounting, banking and creating financial reports, as well as dealing with issues relating to investment, budgets, taxation, currency etc. Much of this information will be commercially sensitive and should only be accessible by the board and the finance team.

Human resources

Next in line comes HR. This team will manage a lot of sensitive and personal information, and so should only be accessible by the HR team and the board. The information will include staff contracts, payroll information, leave records, medical records, identification information, staff appraisals and so forth. This information is both commercially and personally sensitive. It is imperative that the staff's private information is kept securely and access is restricted.

Operations

Operations (OPS) can be subdivided into facilities (FACS) management, IT management (IT) and legal (LGL). You may want to simply create one department with these sub-departments at the outset, or you might, because of the nature of your business, opt to have the three as top-level departments in their own right. For example, if you are managing a large building or portfolio of buildings, like hotels, a high-street chain, or factory, this would merit a top-level department for facilities management. Similarly, with the IT department if you are digitally oriented, such as an e-commerce site or a software service provider.

Operations will probably also be responsible for general business administration and travel; basically things that keep the business ticking along and in many ways provide a backbone from which the departments hang off. This is why you often see chief operating officer or operations director being a key position in a company.

Marketing

Marketing (MKTNG) will be responsible for all corporate branding, publicity, social media, website, brochures and so on. Their activities will include drafting new versions, controlling any changes and keeping the definitive files (such as the corporate logo) readily accessible. They will also be responsible for communicating effectively to the outside world, so will need to set the tone and consistency of the company's message across various print and digital media.

Business development

Business development (BD) is really a pre-sales function for a more complicated business. Clearly you do not need a business development department for a corner shop, but anything that requires finding new customers or partners to drive higher sales perhaps in new or emerging markets will fall in to this category. BD may also be responsible for identifying joint ventures, overseas partners, agents and affiliates.

Sales

There is, of course, much overlap between business development and sales. The sales department is more about the sales execution, upselling and repeat sales. But it needs to know to who business development are already talking and it needs to receive their baton once an opportunity looks promising. Sales will also tend to find new customers in established markets, manage existing clients, maintain price lists and manage more complicated sales projects where, for example, payments depend on a series of delivery milestones. They will also closely monitor the sales pipeline, ensuring leads become qualified and then executed to generate revenue. Obviously, a business lives or dies by its sales, so the sales department is crucial and needs to work closely with marketing, BD, finance and any product development team.

Production

Production (PROD) will manufacture or assemble your products and/ or services that are sold, ensuring quality control and batch records are kept (for example to manage warranty claims, customer returns or even product recalls). The department will also create manuals and data sheets, often in collaboration with marketing (to get the branding right), sales (to get the specifications right) and finance (to get the build costs right).

Research and development

Research and development (R&D) is the department responsible for new product and service creation. At one end of the spectrum, it may be running speculative tests, filing patents, and pioneering new and improved designs. At the other end, it will be tweaking existing products, helping with quality assurance and providing some technical support. This team can be a resource-intensive department, requiring talented and creative people, expensive equipment and a less rigid working environment; all of which can make managing the staff and the process more complicated.

Customer services

Customer Services (CSVS) may also be set up to be separate from sales so as to handle delivery logistics, after-sales support, training and installation. Or for simplicity, it could be part of sales, because this department needs to be aware of customer problems and queries, and can also practice key account management to maintain good relations with important customers and seize repeat sales opportunities.

Sharing data on a server

To mirror the chosen departments, I find it works well to have the folder or directory structure of a shared drive or server arranged to reflect these categories. This is summarized in Table 8.1 with the directory name prefixed by numbers to help define the ordering when listed.

Directory name	Description of contents
00-DOCS	Shared company documents, templates etc from each department for all to access and use.
01-BRD	Board files
02-FIN	Finance department files
03-HR	HR department files
04-OPS	Operations department files
05-MKTNG	Marketing department files
06-BD	Business development department files
07-SALES	Sales department files
08-PROD	Production department files
09-R&D	R&D department files
10-INFO	General resources and information (third-party reports, white papers etc)

Table 8.1. File directories to reflect the corporate structure of departments.

You will also notice two other directories that I have found beneficial. 00-DOCS is the company wide repository for controlled documents and templates, providing a centralized location for the various documents that staff need access to (such as the DN numbered documents). It will also be the location of the document register so that employees are at least aware of all the documents in circulation even if they may not have actual access to their contents. Therefore, as their job function develops or changes, they can request access rather than reinventing a wheel.

Exit warrant

It is much easier to comfort investors or sell your company if all your physical documents are stored logically in a library of files and your digital documents are organized on a server with appropriate access permissions. When you come to promise things during due diligence, you should also be able to find the supporting documents quickly and easily.

The 10-INFO is a suggested company-wide resource of useful information relating to the business. As stated, this could include third-party reports, white papers, links to web pages, news stories, etc. Having this folder available encourages staff not only to drop interesting articles into it, but also to browse through and read things that they may not otherwise have come across. This continuous sharing of knowledge promotes innovation, which can help a company stay fresh and forward looking.

Staffing the departments

The next step is to create the teams of staff that work within the departments. These groups will generally mirror the departments, but depending on your structure and business, some teams will operate within more than one department. Again, at the outset this may all seem rather over the top for a small business, but setting everything up early will help greatly as you recruit and grow. Doing so later when files are located here, there and everywhere will be like untangling an unwieldly knot of multiple twines. So, Table 8.2 summarizes the team structure that aligns with the generic department structure.

Department Name	Description
00-BRD MBRS	Board of directors and chief executives
01-PA to BRD	Personal assistant to the Board Could also include senior C-level management
02-FIN TEAM	Finance department Chief finance officer Accountant Bookkeepers Accounts executives / assistants Procurement Executives / Assistants
03-HR TEAM	HR department HR manager HR executives / assistants
04-OPS TEAM	Operations department Chief information officer / IT Manager Chief operating officer Legal counsel IT executives / assistants Operations executives / assistants Legal executives / assistants
05-MKTNG TEAM	Marketing department Chief marketing officer / marketing manager Marketing executives / assistants Graphics designer
06-BD TEAM	Business development department Business development manager Business development executives / assistants
07-SALES TEAM	Sales department Sales manager Sales executives / assistants Account managers Customers services Helpdesk

08-PROD TEAM	Production department
	Production manager
	Quality assurance and control managers
	Engineers
	Technicians
	Technical helpdesk
09-R&D TEAM	Research and development department
	R&D manager
	R&D scientists / engineers
	Technicians

Table 8.2. Departmental teams to reflect the corporate structure.

Access privileges

Now that you have a structure in place, it is far easier to define and manage permissions for teams to access the company's range of files. This is shown in Table 8.3. Much of it is obvious: the board can access everything; the PA to the board can access all but the board directory; and each department team can access their respective department folder. All the departments can also access the 00-DOCS document repository and the 10-INFO information resource.

Then, there are some additional exceptions which you can tailor for your business, but in the case given as an example below, finance has some limited access to HR, the operations and marketing teams can access a number of departments, the sales and BD teams have some additional access to adjacent departments, and so on.

	00-BRD MBRS	01-PA TO BRD	02-FIN TEAM	03-HR TEAM	04-OPS TEAM	05-MKTNG TEAM	06-BD TEAM	07-SALES TEAM	08-PROD TEAM	09-R&D TEAM
00-DOCS	✓	✓	✓	✓	✓	✓	✓	✓	✓	✓
01-BRD	✓	(✓)								
02-FIN	✓	✓	✓							
03-HR	✓	✓	(✓)	✓						
04-OPS	✓	✓		✓	✓					
05-MKTNG	✓	✓			✓	✓				
06-BD	✓	✓	(✓)		✓		✓			
07-SALES	✓	✓	(✓)		✓	✓	✓	✓		
08-PROD	✓	✓			✓	✓		✓	✓	✓
09-R&D	✓	✓			✓	(✓)	(✓)		(✓)	✓
10-INFO	✓	✓	✓	✓	✓	✓	✓	✓	✓	✓

Table 8.3. A matrix of permissions given to departmental teams to access department files.

These permission structures are all well and good in theory, but how do you do this in reality? Well most computer systems have the ability to manage users and permissions, but to work well you need to invest in either a physical file server or a virtual (cloud-based) file server that has the ability to manage users, user groups, and their associated file permissions. An acronym often used to describe the latter is ACL or Access Control Lists, for example, Windows ACL.

Invaluable capex

By now you'll want to have invested in some company-owned computer hardware and software; most likely a laptop running Microsoft Windows or an Apple Macbook. You will probably need Microsoft Office or to make use of the open source Star Office or Google service. You may wish to use a tablet for convenience and as a way to make simple informal presentations during meetings. Just keep your budget in mind and, if at all possible, make a policy decision on the kind of hardware and software you will use and support within your company. I used to use Windows computers because of their wider choice, lower cost and flexibility. In recent years I have preferred Apple because of the lower risks to malware, the generally higher speed at which they operate (at start-up and shutdown) and the way they integrate well with their other hardware like the iPhone. £1000 broad budget for each IT user

An important thing to note about setting up departments and their access control is that you will retain plenty of flexibility going forward. You can always create new folders, new permissions or change settings as you grow and develop. But the generic structure provides a foundation on which to build and customize for your own case. And the great thing is that new files and folders within the structure can be set to automatically inherit their parent folder's permissions, so new files being placed in a particular location will obtain a default set of properties that are almost certainly correct.

Furthermore, ACL provides additional flexibility in that you can give read-only rights for some groups. Therefore, some departments could have sight of files without being able to edit them. This is another good way to ensure information is efficiently shared throughout your company whilst still ensuring that only the right people can make changes. An example would be a staff handbook that everyone can and should read, but only HR or the board can change.

ACL also enables sub-directories to be given different rights as well, so although the contents of a given department may all be inherited from the overall policy, where certain files need to be worked on collaboratively, the system can allow you to permanently or temporarily alter the access permissions either to groups or individual users.

Sub-folders

As you grow your business, you will have your own range of files pertaining to the nuances of your own operations, but the tables in Appendix A outline some generic sub-folders within each department that I have found useful and logical to start with.

Over time you may wish to control read/write permissions on master files, and a process manager could be the stage gate to allow a new version to be issued. This approach starts to fall in line with ISO standards, such as the ISO 9001 quality management system standard, so will help you be ready for this certification when the time comes.

Take-away and to-do list

- Have a clear outline of your corporate departments and put in place a structure for both physical and digital documents created and used by these respective teams.

- Consider access permissions for these files and directories from the outset.

☐ Create a simple structure of corporate departments.

☐ Create a series of directories on a computer to reflect the departments.

☐ Set up a list of department teams.

☐ Create a matrix of permissions outlining which teams can access the folders.

☐ Create a series of sub-directories.

9.

VIRTUAL IS THE NEW REALITY

IT complexity

Computers, those great labour-saving devices, can cause all kinds of problems. They need passwords, they use different operating systems (Mac or Windows, for example), and they need updating and managing. Then, add to that your smart phone and tablet, and the fact that your growing staff base also each need their own IT provisions and you can see that this could soon get out of hand. Especially if you are not particularly IT literate yourself.

We will talk a bit more about cyber security later, but there are also some other basic things to get right with IT. First of all, you need to manage what devices have access to what parts of your business.

Company email

Each member of staff will have an email address. To scale, it is better to start using a format with a first name and surname from the outset, rather than just a forename. The latter may seem less formal, but a growing company will soon have more than one Jane or John. Only go for firstname@ if you are embarking on a lifestyle business where you envisage just a few employees, and then only if you really must.

A common format is of course firstname.surname@yourcompany, and where you have more than one you could add a number, eg, john.smith2@. Some companies prefer less guessable formats to cut down on spam or unsolicited enquiries, so adding a number can help, or using middle initials, so that formats may be firstname-lastname@, ablastname@, firstname.a.lastname1234@ etc. Whatever you decide, check that it is logical and not too cumbersome, then roll it out.

Additionally, it is also useful for each department to have one or more generic email based on function that can be monitored by or forwarded to a specific individually internally. This helps to deal with issues of staff changing job role or moving on. The table below outlines some good examples that you could implement from early on, which would appear on the templates of key documents like invoices, staff policies and product warranties.

Department	Suggested generic emails
01-BRD	board@yourcompany.com MD@yourcompany.com or CEO@yourcompany.com PA@yourcompany.com
02-FIN	finance@yourcompany.com
03-HR	HR@yourcompany.com
04-OPS	operations@yourcompany.com IT@yourcompany.com traveldesk@yourcompany.com legal@yourcompany.com
05-MKTNG	marketing@yourcompany.com
06-BD	BD@yourcompany.com
07-SALES	sales@yourcompany.com customerservices@yourcompany.com or services@yourcompany.com
08-PROD	production@yourcompany.com
09-R&D	RnD@yourcompany.com

Table 9.1. Generic emails aligned with company departments.

Most internet service providers will allow you to set email aliases and forwarding, so you do not necessarily need an email account for each of the addresses given in Table 9.1. They can just be set as redirects; probably to you at the beginning, but then you can forward them to colleagues as you recruit and new job functions and responsibilities are delegated.

The advantage of this system is that you can set up templates and print documents with the generic emails on (such as invoices, terms and conditions etc), then not worry about changing them as the staff base changes. Furthermore, as staff come and go in the future, you can simply redirect the generic emails to the appropriate successor. It should also be possible to copy yourself or a senior management colleague in on some of the redirects so that you can monitor enquiries and help train new staff to respond appropriately.

With emails, you also want to manage out of office, footers and disclaimers, and viruses. Ideally, you will have an out-of-office policy in terms of who to contact for different people. It is also important to have a company-wide footer and disclaimer on your email as a template for people to add their name, job title, address and contact details. The latter will be personalized for each account, but your email provider may well enable you to set global footers which could include reference to confidential information, the wrong recipient and your company number etc. A sample footer text is given below in Figure 9.1. and it can be useful to create one and lock it in a controlled document using the DN notation as a template so that everyone uses the same version.

Prospective investors and potential acquirers will like to see that you have taken care of email footers in this way, because it demonstrates that you are concerned about confidential information and liabilities to third parties.

Confidentiality

This email is sent on behalf of MyCo Ltd. Its contents and any attachments may contain confidential information and may be legally privileged. If you are not the intended recipient or addressee you should not copy, print, store or forward this email or any attachments. Please notify the sender immediately and then permanently delete the email and any attachments from your system.

Disclaimer

Although this email and attachments have been scanned for viruses and malware, MyCo accepts no liability for any loss or damage arising from the receipt, any use of this communication, or for any liability arising from its content. Please do not open any suspicious attachments.

Monitoring of Email

MyCo may monitor the emails for security and for lawful business purposes.

Company information

Company number 1234567; registered in England and Wales. VAT number 123456789.

Figure 9.1. Sample email footer content for all email from the organization.

Data storage

The next point to consider is how you will store and access all your data. We began thinking about this when a list of proposed directories for computer files were described and a permission structure was tabulated based on departments.

The good news is that once you create a working structure, this can be migrated to different platforms as you expand, so nothing need to be set in stone.

If you go down the cloud route, you may consider services such as Windows 365 or Google Drive in which to set up the system. The advantage is that these are evolving services, backed up, and remotely accessible from pretty much anywhere enabling you and your staff to stay connected when travelling or working from home. The disadvantage is that you may need to pay recurring subscription fees, you need (good) internet connectivity and there could be issues around security and privacy; more on this later, but you are parking very sensitive corporate information with another company and you may need to know in which country (or countries) the data actually resides.

As such, I have always invested in a physical server to sit in a locked cupboard on our premises. These days, ones suitable for a small enterprise are the price of a midrange desktop computer and have an intuitive user interface. I have had experience with Windows SharePoint but recently I have used Synology servers which have user friendly software, an advanced ACL capability, the ability to encrypt the file system, and seem to have a good grasp of the importance of cyber security in general.

As well as good quality hard drives, use a drive array (either two disks which effectively means that one disk mirrors the other and you have two copies of the data) or a RAID array (which means typically four disks share the information in such a way that multiple drives can fail and be swopped out without interrupting work). This may not sound important in the beginning, but once you have a team of people working, it can be problematic to interrupt the IT services that everyone has come to rely on.

Physical servers on your premises will put less demand on the external bandwidth to a cloud server, and you could still back up to a cloud service or another off-site server under your own control out of working hours when internet bandwidth is better.

Invaluable capex

A server with software that allows you to manage groups, users and access provisions on your network is now invaluable. You could opt for a cloud-based service and pay a growing monthly fee as you use more resources and features, or you could buy your own hardware and install it on your premises. I favour the latter in the early days, as it means you have full control of your data and know where it is residing. £600 for a hardware server or £20–£50 per month for a service

---

It is also highly recommended that you ensure that the data on the server is encrypted so that should it be partially hacked or stolen, the data is still protected. This also goes for the back-ups, particularly as these files could be on removable hard drives or remote servers. In the case of the former, their transportation offsite (eg, to your home) poses a risk of loss.

I have wrestled over the years to create a robust, inexpensive, scalable server system for our businesses that does not rely on me remembering to back up or rotate disk drives between home and work. It has taken a little bit of research, but Figure 9.2 shows three examples that could be adopted, and the latter is the most complex but the one I have now adopted for my current businesses.

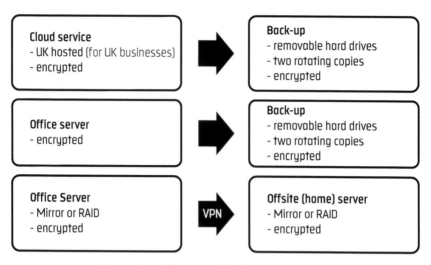

Figure 9.2. Possible server and back-up schemes to adopt.

The point is that as long as you have thought about the process and have something that works, you can always improve and adapt as your company grows. Eventually, you will have a Chief Information Officer (CIO) or equivalent whose job it will be to ensure the IT system is robust, secure and backed up. They will be able adapt what you have started. For example, it is worth having some monthly back-ups that are kept and not re-written, as these provide recoverable snapshots from a while back and may help avoid problems with nasty malware. Cryptolocker, for example, tries to encrypt files even on connected back-up disks and force the payment of a ransom to unlock them.

It is also important not to scatter your information all over the place. Do not start using multiple online (cloud) services and then lose sight of them. If a service is no good after you have tried it, remove your data and ensure your staff know that it is no longer to be used. Otherwise you could have important or sensitive information in places that are not being backed up, are susceptible to being compromised, or do not align with the current policies in your business.

Remote access

The latter option in Figure 9.2 introduces the VPN or virtual private network. This is another important consideration to enable you and co-

90

workers to access files remotely and is particularly important if you want to access information from a non-secure location such as a café, airport, train or hotel.

To set up a VPN will generally require a midrange internet gateway (the box you may normally acquire from your internet service provider to access the internet and provide wifi). Paying a few hundred pounds for one will give more robust features, such as the ability to create virtual local area networks (for a guest network to be separated from your main office network) and VPNs. They may also enable you to have more than one internet enabled phone line into your premises so that the load can be shared and if one line goes down, the system switches to the other (hopefully still) working line automatically. These systems will become more useful as your business grows and interruptions become more expensive.

Given all of this, the system I have set up enables me to operate securely from home and the office, whilst also ensuring offsite back-ups are maintained. This is summarized in Figure 9.3.

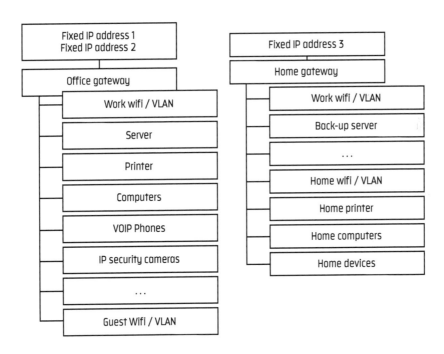

Figure 9.3. Small office / home office (SOHO) network.

If you have followed the story to this stage, you now have a scalable email system, a scalable computer filing system, a way of sharing files appropriately, a way of accessing files securely from home and away, and a back-up system to prevent file loss due to theft, fire or corruption.

Disaster recovery

This means you have also started to consider a disaster recovery plan (DRP) in as much that you are starting to build in resilience to your electronic files that reduces the chance of disaster and has in place some rescue options such as a remote back-up. The DRP is an important evolving contingency that will hopefully be written down and updated. As such, you can create a document MyCo-CC-DN000x.1 Disaster Recovery Plan, and, under the heading of data, describe the measures you have put in place. Investors will really like to see this attention to detail.

Telephony

Another key consideration is your business phone number and how you will manage extensions as your organization grows. In a serviced business centre, you may be offered a number on their system, and it may be an ISDN bundle which means you will not be able to take the telephone number with you when you move on. This is a serious concern because changing a business phone number will result in lost sales and potentially disgruntled customers who are unable to reach you. Changing your phone number on all your business cards, letterheads, marketing collateral and wherever it appears online is also time consuming and costly.

It would be much better to have control of the phone line yourself or to use a virtual telephony service such as voice over internet protocol (VoIP). In the latter case, you should be able to add numbers and extensions as you grow and make use of the internet to handle your calls. This can sometimes mean call quality will be lower, but if you have a good internet connection and either a dedicated line for VoIP calls or some hardware that can prioritize the call data, the system can work well, will be low cost and, most importantly, scalable.

This virtual telephony system also means that you can usually add phone numbers that are not in your geographical area, so you may select a London, Birmingham or Manchester phone number in the UK for example to give your business more credence in a specific area. You could also select certain numbers for certain departments early on, for example, a reception number, a sales number and a number for you. The extension concept also means you can flexibly forward calls from specific numbers to different people in your organization to cover for holidays, changes in staff and so on.

In the business centre that I co-founded in Malvern, I stumbled across VoIP telephony having already booked for an ISDN line to be installed. Luckily, we went the VoIP route despite paying for the committed ISDN installation, because the result has been a flexible system in which our resident businesses have been able to bring in and port out their own number seamlessly, resulting in no disruption to their business. We have also been able to gradually grow the number of phone extensions used in our business as the staff size has increased.

Digital office

Having a paperless office is an oft-quoted goal, but it is hard to achieve. Firstly, you will need to scan hard-copy documents and decide whether to keep the hard copies as well. I take the view that accounts need paper copies filed, such as receipts and invoices, as often the accountant will want to see them, and tax authorities do usually stipulate that records are kept for several years. Some online accounting software will arrange to scan all your receipts as part of their service. You could certainly do it yourself, but it will take time, which may be better spent on other tasks.

Electronic records also need to be backed up carefully and in multiple versions, as it is all too easy to erase an electronic file (and not even notice) or for malware like ransomware to encrypt or erase files (and, as mentioned previously, even those files on connected back-up systems).

On the server, I find a useful way to name and store files is to prefix them with the date so a file name has the following format: YYYYMMDD-filename. This then orders all the documents by name in a folder based on their date, and enables you to find something quickly based on when it was likely to have been done or to follow a story (for example in business development). If everyone in the company adopts the same system, it is easy for people to find where things have got to.

Emails are particularly problematic, because they tend to be linked to a person and can reside on their computer or in their mail software. I encourage users to drag important emails into the server's file system and prefix them with their date as above. To facilitate this process, it is actually possible to write a little Microsoft Macro or Apple Automator script to prefix a file with the date there and then by just dropping it on an icon.

Software tools

The other way to make the most of IT is to use software systems for each of your departments that also facilitate cross-department and companywide collaboration. Table 9.2 indicates some possibilities, and some of these may be internally held licenses (ie, software installed on your own set of computers and server) or cloud based (provided remotely by a service provider).

Some of these software tools will enable a few of the directories discussed previously to be avoided; for example, BD contacts and SALES contacts could all be managed through a CRM system. However, the important point is that you can always choose a specific piece of software to migrate to later and all the relevant information will be to hand. Once you adopt new software, you need to spend a bit of time aligning the system, archiving the legacy data and being sure the new system is operating correctly.

Department	Software services
01-BRD	Will need access to all services listed below
02-FIN	Accounting (eg, Quickbooks, Sage, MYOB, Xero) Enterprise resource planning (ERP, eg, SAP, Oracle, Odoo) extends accounting to other services such as staff management, purchasing, production planning and sales.
03-HR	Payroll software (eg, Basic PAYE) Staff management software (eg, BambooHR, HRMatrix, WebHR) Aspects of an ERP system where used
04-OPS	Aspects of an ERP system where used
05-MKTNG	Online marketing software (eg, Mailchimp, Constant Contact) Online event software (eg, Eventbrite) Social networks and associated management tools (eg, Tweetdeck, Hootsuite etc) Aspects of an ERP system where used
06-BD	Customer relationship management (CRM) software Aspects of an ERP system where used
07-SALES	CRM software Sales pipeline management software Aspects of an ERP system where used
08-PROD	Project management software (eg, Microsoft Project) Aspects of an ERP system where used Computer Aided Design (eg, AutoCAD)
09-R&D	Project management software (eg, Microsoft Project) Aspects of an ERP system where used Computer Aided Design (eg, AutoCAD)

Table 9.2. Example software used by different departments.

There are also numerous productivity software tools and applications that can be used across teams to keep communication flowing by making announcements, creating collaborations and sharing resources. Examples include Basecamp and Slack, but there are many others. The thing to watch is that they store information in the cloud and require users to login from their computers or phones. This means you do not have full control on the data, and if it is sensitive or confidential, it may be unwise to rely on a remote third-party service. That said, these services are so slick, intuitive and low cost (or even free) that they can bring lots of benefit to your business and some staff may really take to the platform.

Therefore, try to keep track on the services being used (or delegate this task to operations or IT) and limit it to a few that you can leverage the most value without dispersing your data widely and having too many options to worry about.

The best way to start this process is to create a simple document or spreadsheet in the IT department that lists both the hardware and software in use within the company. In terms of the hardware, it could include the specifications like CPU and memory, the make and model, who is using it and where it is located. This list should include all hardware such as routers, switches, wifi access points, printers, cameras, IP phones and indeed other internet of things (IoT) devices, as you want to know all the equipment that is managed by you and connected to your network. We will discuss more about the complications of personal devices later.

The software list should indicate specific software installed on particular machines, including the version number and license number or certificate of authentication. A list should also be maintained of the remote cloud-based software services in use, and who the administrator(s) are for these services.

Backing up across the team

It is at this point that you also need to have back-up policies and procedures in place for all these different devices and services. Laptops and computers should be backing up to your network server regularly using back-up software like Time Machine on Apple computers. You will also want to download and file configuration files where available for the devices as well (such as routers) so that they can be reset easily in the future. Online services also need to be assessed in terms of creating local back-ups so that data can be restored or indeed moved to another service provider if things do not work out.

Exit warrant

Potential investors and acquirers will be concerned about the integrity and security of your company data, who has access to what, and how well organized it is. You need to be able show that you have taken care over how personal and customer data is managed, how company data is organized and shared, and what software licenses you have to use. They will also be keen to see that a system is scalable, not reliant on a single obscure service provider, and not in need of a major overhaul before the business can grow further.

As you can see, there is a lot to think about, and IT is particularly difficult because it is the backbone to the entire business and yet much of it is invisible. It is often taken for granted and many aspects work on settings that may be wholly unsuited to a robust and secure business environment.

Take-away and to-do list

- Set up your business communications like email and phone numbers with the future in mind so that you have a scalable system.

- Use a company server for all your files and data that has been set up with suitable access permissions, a back-up policy and encryption.

- Be selective with software services so that you know what is being used and data is not lost or compromised in the future.

☐ Set up personal email addresses using a standard system, such as firstname.lastname.

☐ Set up a series of generic email addresses for each department or job function.

☐ Put in place a fileserver either as hardware or a cloud-based service.

☐ Create regular data back-ups based on a schedule.

☐ Provide a company VPN service for remote access and improved security in the field.

☐ Set up company phone number(s).

☐ Create a list of hardware, software and cloud-based services in use within the company.

10.

BUSINESS AGREEMENTS
AND DISAGREEMENTS

Understanding what you are agreeing to

Your first executed agreements with a third party are likely to be with an accountant or with the landlord of a premises, so what system should you put in place to handle these documents with an eye to the future?

Firstly, read them and check you can indeed agree with them. It is amazing how many people assume an agreement from a company that does a lot of business must produce amicable agreements. There could easily be clauses in the document that are untenable or need adjusting for your situation. Check that notice periods, termination conditions, payment details and so on are all acceptable. Agreements that centre around collaboration and the use and sharing of intellectual property can be particularly troubling, because they may try to grab rights about ownership and use that are certainly not in your best interest and moreover could be detrimental to your business.

Remember it is not just you stomaching the deal. You need to consider whether your business successor could agree to them too, and if not, are there sufficient escape clauses to terminate or renegotiate? A simple example would be a lease agreement. If you sign up to a five-year lease and you suddenly have the opportunity to sell your business in a year's time because of where you are with the growth of your business, are the acquirers going to be happy with the arrangement? They may have their own business premises in another part of the country, for example. Therefore, in this case, you may want to insert a break clause that occurs if the company is sold or secures a certain level of investment. The lessor will probably want something in return for this, so negotiate a sensible break fee. It will be much easier to agree such a provision early on before the trigger actually happens, as the lessor will see it as an unlikely event and they will also be keen to have you sign the lease.

In general, it is always easier to negotiate smaller termination penalties before signing an agreement; a good approach is to explain that there may be situations where your business will need to expand or contract, so the agreement (whatever it is, not just a property lease) would need a termination clause perhaps with a few months' fees by way of compensation.

When you execute an agreement, always make sure you retain a signed and dated original (or at the very least a good quality copy). Today agreements are sometimes handled online by a web-based service, so be sure to download a copy for your own records, so you are not relying on the service continuing to operate.

A system for filing and tracking signed agreements

Next comes the system to keep track of these important signed documents, whether a physical original or one signed online and available only as a virtual file. A simple approach is to give them a serial number along the lines of an asset or a document number. Indeed, in many ways agreements are assets (or liabilities); they are securing you a service or securing you a customer, and they certainly have value or a necessity to the business otherwise why would you be signing them? They are also documents, but the DN notation introduced earlier is really reserved for your own master documents and templates rather than signed agreements.

Therefore, a system that I have found to work well is to write on the original, or label the electronic file, using a similar nomenclature, but instead use SA (for signed agreements) as the acronym: MyCo-CC-SA000x.y. Do not try to label drafts like this, only final versions of agreements that are to be signed. They are not signed agreements until all the signatures are there; and that is important. Also, there are not really version numbers of signed documents, but in the unlikely event that an agreement is superseded, you have the .y version number available in the system. Having said all that, do keep the drafts on file as well, as you can refer back to them as necessary. The history of an agreement may be useful in the future if, for example, there is an issue of interpretation. Arbitration or a court may use early drafts to establish the intention of an agreement, and whether the contentious issue had in fact been discussed between versions. The evidence could be in your favour, so it is well keeping it to hand.

The simple system described will enable you to keep track of all executed agreements. These are important for running your business and also for future due diligence when you come to raise finance or sell the business. Potential investors or acquirers will want to see what agreements are in place; both in terms of the positive aspect of who has committed to provide you with value, but also what liabilities you have accrued and when they cease.

Invaluable capex

If you have not already invested in an office printer and scanner, now might be the time to do so, as you can print hard copies of agreements to sign and scan copies of executed agreements, so you can store them on your server and back them up remotely. £150-£300 for a midrange all-in-one inkjet printer.

Your accountant will also need to be aware of your agreements because some of the liabilities (like minimum payments or fixed-term contracts) may need to be added to your balance sheet to give a fair view of all your company's assets and liabilities.

Your catalogue of signed agreements can be further enhanced if the index file logs a few pertinent bits of information. A useful index includes: the SA number; the agreement title or type (such as property lease or non-disclosure agreement); the counterparty (or who else signed the agreement); and dates for review, expiry and renewal. You could also include a brief description or, more usefully, a few notes about the negotiation and the important clauses. Then, when you come back to them you are instantly reminded of the key things you considered when signing the original agreement. This filing system can also be useful when your team grows, because a colleague can make use of the summary information when negotiating a future transaction..

My Company Ltd Register of signed agreements					
MyCo-CC-SAxxxx.y					
SA	Title	Signed by	Signed with	Expiry date	Notes
0001	Shareholder agreement	A. Person			
0002	Office lease	A. Person			
0003	NDA with company X	A. Person			
0004	Telephone service agreement	A. Person			

Figure 10.1. A register of signed agreements.

There will also be situations where you are the originator of agreements, particularly as you grow and start to 'call the shots' for others. An example would be your own sales agreement, a non-disclosure agreement or perhaps a software license agreement. In this situation, you would use the DN system to keep control of the template or master document, but when a version is completed or modified and then signed with a specific organization, that executed document is then itself logged using the SA system. The advantage of this is that you can include a footer that says 'agreement based on DN-MyCo-CC xxxx.1', so that you know from which template it was derived. As such, the SA index notes section discussed above could also highlight any major departures from the DN template; for example, a six-year non-disclosure agreement rather than a standard five-year clause.

Keeping legal costs down

Drafting your own set of agreements, and reviewing those of others, can be an expensive task when you engage your own legal counsel. However, unless you are a trained lawyer, it is always wise to get these documents done properly. There are ways to save time and money, however. Firstly, in terms of drafting, try to create your own term sheet first containing the important provisions from which your lawyer can draft an agreement and add all the boilerplate clauses. Also, do use the internet to find example templates from which you can base your own agreements. However, do beware that they could have outdated provisions that do not relate to the most recent laws, and do be sure that the templates relate to the country or jurisdiction that you are operating in (a US agreement will not generally stand up in a UK court of law for example).

If you can do much of the legwork yourself, your own lawyer will have a lot less to do. You could even ask your lawyer for one of their own off-the-shelf templates to review and mark up. That way, they will be familiar with the structure and you can save their time and hence reduce their costs.

The same goes for reviewing agreements. If you are asked to sign another party's agreement, read it through and check the headline specifics are suitable for you. You can then explain to your lawyer that you are happy with the commercial terms but you want them to review the document for catches and weasel wording that might not be in your best interest. More importantly, they might be able to make some of the clauses mutual or add a few protective provisions that are in your interest. For example, something to help with arbitration or ensure you can terminate in a penalty-free and timely manner should you need to do so.

A classic example of understanding legalese from my experience is if a party asks you to make 'best efforts' to do something, such as generate sales or respond to their support requests. This simple innocuous looking two-word phrase can be quite onerous; it was explained to me as 'leaving no stone unturned' in your endeavours. If applied to a marketing activity, it could mean you and your staff have to go around with a sandwich board over their shoulders advertising the goods. This is probably not what you had in mind.

However, making 'reasonable efforts' is probably more palatable, and if they complain when you suggest the amendment, you know that they may have unrealistic expectations of you that will not bode well in the future.

Legal agreements often have lots of sections and a number of general provisions called boilerplates. Some of this can be hard to read and understand, but doing so is a necessity as lawyers will often put it all in for good measure and it may have ramifications for you in the future.

For example, be aware of clauses relating to 'successors and assigns'. These usually outline that a contract cannot be transferred to a new assignee or a new owner of the company. However, if you are growing a business with a view to an exit, it would be good to ensure that contracts and agreements will still apply to a new owner, as the contracts will form part of the value of the company and having to renegotiate will cost both time and money, and may well result in the loss of a key contract or the worsening of terms. Some contracts will be less crucial than others, but licence agreements are a good example as these give the company a right to do something and may be detrimental if no longer applicable after an exit.

Exit warrant

Make sure all the agreements you have ever signed are catalogued, filed and available. Investors and potential acquirers will want to be sure what liabilities they have, and they will ask you to underwrite them insofar as any undisclosed liabilities will become your problem. Due diligence will also seek to ensure that valuable agreements that are in place do not prematurely terminate or fall away when the company is sold, merged or changes ownership.

A good example of how the incorrect use of boilerplate can result in a legal mess is the documented case between Oxonica and Neuftec. Their agreement contained some ambiguities that came about through poor drafting and the 'bolting together of legal boilerplate' without proper thought about the legalese and interpretation. The upshot was that a case was lost because the court had to make a judgement on the interpretation and scope of the agreement. You can search the internet for reports on this case and see what a minefield awaits when poorly written agreements are hauled up in court for dissection.

Internal processes to handle agreements

Building your own arsenal of standard templates early on can be a good strategy, as this way you will be familiar with the overall agreement that you are signing up to, and the other party will need to spend time (and probably their own money) undertaking the review. Examples of the kind of agreements to have on tap are:

- non-disclosure agreements (NDAs or confidentiality agreements);

- collaboration agreements;

- consulting agreements;

- memorandums of understanding (MoUs);

- and letters of intent (LoIs).

In the case of non-disclosure agreements, it is also worth having a number of subtly different variants: a standard mutual agreement where both parties will share confidential information; a one-way agreement where you will be sharing information; and one aimed at an individual such as a consultant or employee, rather than a commercial entity.

It is also worth having boxes in the footer of each page for each signatory to initial, thus demonstrating both you and they have read and agreed to each individual page.

Another important consideration is who is authorised to sign agreements and at what point should the board be convened to do so.

A good way is to add this information to your own agreements; so, for example, a non-disclosure agreement may state that it is only to be signed by a director of the company.

The other approach is to keep a master list of permissions based on category and contract value. As such, only a director may be permitted to sign an agreement where the liability or contract value exceeds a certain amount of money. In the early stages, however, it is often prudent to ensure all agreements are signed by you as a founder, or an executive co-director, and slowly roll out well-defined exceptions such as NDAs for the technical manager or personal employment contracts for the HR manager.

The same considerations apply to modifying the terms of the agreement; such modifications will almost certainly need a director to agree depending on the nature of the variation.

All eventualities cannot be predicted, so rather than trying to write a catch-all policy, the intention should be to have a system in place that catalogues agreements, highlights changes and enables simple exceptions to be allowed to avoid bottlenecks. Remember that one of your aims is to delegate routine tasks and decisions so you will need to ensure that policies are in place to enable this to happen.

One area where you will generate a lot of paperwork is with respect to employees and their employment contracts or service agreements. However, the same systems can be applied; a DN number can be used for the master template with blank salary, benefits and job description. Then, the final executed version for a specific employee can be catalogued using the SA system, held confidentially in the HR files.

What this demonstrates is that not everyone in the company should be able to see all the agreements. Indeed, agreements can have commercially sensitive or personally private information. So ideally the index document should be visible to everyone in the company and could be located in the 00-DOCS directory. This will enable people to generate, find or use documents, and issue a new one with a new number as appropriate. However, avoid writing any sensitive information in the description field of the index and the agreements themselves will need to have limited (possibly very limited) access.

Take-away and to-do list

- Read all agreements carefully before signing them.

- Maintain a policy of who can sign agreements.

- Keep an index and filing system of templates and final version (signed) agreements.

- Be mindful of the sensitive nature of the contents of many agreements and use the permission-based filing system for best effect.

☐ Start numbering all your signed agreements using the MyCo-CC-SAxxxx.y nomenclature.

☐ Build up an arsenal of agreement templates within the MyCo-CC-DNxxxx.y scheme.

11.

ACCOUNTING THE BEANS

Watching the cashflow

You have heard the saying that 'cash is king', which boils down to having enough money in the bank to cope with your business expenses and growth at any given moment in time. Many things interfere with this simple plan; customers do not pay on time, suppliers need paying before you've shipped the goods to your own customers, and R&D is expensive. And if you are VAT registered (or equivalent), you may need to pay the VAT bill from invoices raised before the VAT has been collected from your own customers.

The main task is therefore to keep a close eye on the financials and to understand where the fixed, ongoing costs are, and who still owes you money. At the very least you should be checking your accounts in detail on a monthly basis.

I am in the habit of keeping the bookkeeping up to date and then having a balance sheet, profit-and-loss statement, and debtors-ageing summary generated on a monthly basis. Then, rather than just filing it away, I take a short amount of time to look at each item and see how it compares to the previous month. Is everything comparable and where there are significant differences, can they be explained? Moreover, are the people that owe you money from last month now off the list?

As the business grows, you can delegate your bookkeeper, accountant or financial controller to generate these reports each month. If you have regular board meetings, this is the time to table the statements, but if not, then at least sit down with someone like the bookkeeper and / or co-director to review the finances systematically.

An accounting system that brings benefit

Having a system in place for your accounts is not only necessary for compliance, as the taxman could visit at any time to check you are keeping accurate records, but also for your own peace of mind that the business is in order. Furthermore, should an investor or potential acquirer ask you about your general finances, for example in the early stages of a negotiation, you will be familiar with them. And you will likely be able to answer simple questions like: what is your monthly burn rate? how much money is in the bank? what is your largest monthly expense? what is this financial year's gross profit and net profit likely to be?

The system I have adopted is to create a number of sections in a lever arch file for a financial year (or files as the year progresses and the paperwork builds up). The sections are:

- invoices (ie, invoices raised to generate income from customers);

- company expenses (ie, invoices from third parties that are business costs and purchases);

- petty cash;

- staff expenses;

- bank statements;

- accounts (management and end of year);

- and tax (information about both VAT and corporation tax as appropriate).

The process involves filing the paperwork in order, based on the date of the invoice being raised. For clarity, in our businesses we highlight the date with a fluorescent marker and then add a note to indicate that the transaction is added to the accounts in our accounting software.

So, as we tend to use Quickbooks accounting software, the initials QB are written on the paper copy.

These transactions are reconciled against the bank statement when it arrives thus ensuring some paperwork exists for each transaction (it is more difficult these days because things can be purchased online and direct debits can result in transactions without immediately accessible supporting documents).

As part of the reconciliation process, I have the date that it cleared the bank account written on the paperwork as well. This is really helpful when checking back, as it means it is easier to sort out rogue transactions or cross-check when there is a query.

To keep on top of this, we also have a monthly checklist, as shown in Table 11.1. This is completed by the bookkeeper each month, and then I sit down with him or her and check there is nothing unusual. I then run through the month's accounts satisfying myself that everything is correct (particularly that expenses are posted to the correct account category) and that VAT, where applicable, is accurately recorded.

Actions (AS = accounting software)	Done (Bookkpr)	Chkd (MD)
Company invoices		
• Invoices generated in AS with correct sales code and VAT if applicable. Printed invoice date highlighted, AS and bookkeeper's initials written on paper copy, then filed in the invoice section of accounts folder in date order.	☐	☐
• Any remittance notes, additional related documents or earlier invoice versions stapled behind the invoice.	☐	☐

Actions (AS = accounting software)	Done (Bookkpr)	Chkd (MD)
Company expenses (purchases)		
• Printed purchases received and entered in AS with correct account code and VAT if applicable. Purchase date (their invoice date) highlighted, AS & bookkeeper's initials written on paper copy, then filed in the expenses section of accounts folder in date order.	☐	☐
• Any delivery notes, additional related documents or quotations stapled behind the expense.	☐	☐
Petty cash		
• Final balance matches with the petty cash tin. All receipts arranged on additional sheets, numbered consecutively and attached.	☐	☐
• Entered details in AS, using correct account codes and VAT if applicable. Written AS and bookkeeper's initials on sheet and filed in petty-cash section of accounts folder.	☐	☐
Staff expenses		
• All receipts arranged on additional sheets, numbered consecutively and attached.	☐	☐
• Returned to director to check and make payment.	☐	☐
• Details entered in AS using correct account codes and VAT if applicable. Signed 'processed by' section, written AS on sheet and filed in staff-expenses section of accounts folder.	☐	☐

Actions (AS = accounting software)	Done (Bookkpr)	Chkd (MD)
Bank reconciliation		
• Bank statement received and each transaction supported with paper copy in sections above. Each supported entry ticked on statement. 'cleared [date]' written on paper copy.	☐	☐
• All unsupported transactions queried and rectified. Use paper notifications for direct debits, payroll etc.	☐	☐
• Uncleared items verified, eg, different company or personal expense?	☐	☐
• Bank reconciled on AS with interest and bank fees added where applicable. Bank reconciliation report printed.	☐	☐
• Bank and reconciliation statements filed in bank section of accounts folder.	☐	☐
Management accounts review		
• Balance sheet dated end of month printed, profit and loss for month printed. Profit-and-loss year to end of month printed. Ageing summary printed. VAT monitor sheet update if applicable. This form completed.	☐	☐
• Sit-down review to check monthly figures and any issues.	☐	☐
• Accounting documents and this form filed in accounts section of accounts folder.	☐	☐
Quarterly VAT submission (if applicable)		
• No outstanding issues at the end of the quarter and director checked above for each of the three months.	☐	☐
• VAT report printed and ready for processing.	☐	☐
• Director to check, file online and process in AS.	☐	☐

Table 11.1. An example monthly bookkeeping and accounting checklist that ensures all the financial records are organized and complete.

Making time to do this is crucial, and actually does not take long for a small medium business once you get going. It is a really good way to stay on top of your finances and see where money is being spent and who your good and bad customers (from both a sales size and a prompt payment point of view) are.

Structure of company accounts

In terms of accounting software for the company, there are plenty of options available, and your accountant will probably recommend something based on their own experience. There are a few things to consider. Firstly, make sure the software supports the country you are operating in; it is not just having the right currency symbol, but also supporting other aspects of your business' finances in the correct way for the territory (such as VAT and payroll). You may also want to consider whether to use a system installed on your computer or a cloud-based system that is accessed through the internet. The latter is becoming favoured because it is available to view and update even on the road, but there are issues around security that need to be understood as well.

Invaluable capex

Select a good-quality flexible accounting package that will grow with your company. Examples include Quickbooks, Sage, MYOB and Xero. £100–£200 standalone software or a service £15–£25 per month.

When you (or your accountant) set up your accounts, be sure you understand the system; for example, the account categories that various income and expenses will be posted to, and what their scope is. This will ensure consistency in the management accounts and less time spent reworking the accounts at year end when everything needs to be sorted for filing.

Another key aspect is to separate out your operating overheads (things you will need to pay to exist and grow your business in general) and those expenses that relate to supplying your products and services. This will enable you to clearly see your gross profit (the profit on your products or services before taking into account the overheads) and your operating profit (the profit after all the expenses). This way you can understand your cashflow better; what is the burn rate of an early stage business and how is it impacted by winning more customers and supplying more products or services. These aspects can have different effects on your cashflow and may not be immediately intuitive.

Table 11.2 gives a list of accounts that might be useful for a company, highlighting the classes of sales, assets, liabilities, and expenses along with some notes about what to watch for as your company grows. The numbering system of account codes is given by way of example, to show how similar items are grouped and ordered in a hierarchy.

Account code and description	Notes
1000 · CASH / BANK 1010 · Bank current account 1020 · Petty cash 1030 · Credit card 1040 · Other account (eg, Paypal) 1050 · Bank savings account	Keeping track of your cash situation is of paramount importance. Keep petty cash to a minimum and have a record sheet to log its use. Treat other accounts as line items as well, and if you do have a cash surplus, look into savings accounts just as you might with your personal finances.
1500 · ACCOUNTS RECEIVABLE	Ensuring your customers pay quickly is also important, so keep an eye on this section to see what money you are still owed.
2000 · OTHER CURRENT ASSET 2100 · Undeposited funds 2200 · Stock	Try to minimise stock and keep an eye on its real value; outdated stock may never sell.

Account code and description	Notes
3000 · FIXED ASSETS 3100 · Furniture 3200 · Office equipment 3300 · Accumulated depreciation	Bear in mind that assets can make a balance sheet look strong but greatly affect the cashflow of your business. For example, if you use sales income to buy a large asset that depreciates over several years, your profit and loss in terms of accruals accounting is unlikely to reflect your cash accounting situation as indicated by your bank balance.
4000 · ACCOUNTS PAYABLE	Here you need to watch growing liabilities of what you owe others. As your company grows, so monthly accounts payable relating to contracts can become sizeable and if you are unable to service the debts when they become due, you are insolvent.
5000 · OTHER CURRENT LIABILITY 5100 · Loan account 5200 · Director loan account 5300 · Customer deposits 5400 · VAT liability	There are often many liabilities in your business, and as you grow, the variety increases too. You may have loans, deposits and tax liabilities beyond just more traditional trading expenses.
6000 · EQUITY 6100 · Share capital account 6200 · Retained earnings	Ultimately, as you aim for an exit, you will be wanting to sell equity. But the balance sheet value of the equity will almost certainly be much smaller than the value you can extract, because this tends to show only historical paid up share value which may be based on par value.
7000 · INCOME 7100 · Product sales 7200 · Project management/ consulting 7300 · Grant 7400 · Interest income	A key section of your accounts, as this is where you can see your sales revenue and other sources of income. Try to understand the breakdown; is it mainly lumpy grant income, smooth sales of a particular product or one-off large project sales that are contributing to your top line.

Account code and description	Notes
8000 · COST OF SALES 8100 · Bill of materials	This section is often poorly understood by early-stage businesses because they tend to put their costs of sales against overhead expenses. If you can identify the real costs of things that you spend that make up a product or service, it greatly helps to shed light on your business.

9000 · OVERHEADS
  9100 · EMPLOYEE COSTS
    9110 · Salaries and wages
    9112 · PAYE salaries
    9114 · Pension contributions
    9116 · Casual labour
    9118 · PAYE taxation
    9120 · Motor expenses
    9122 · Car mileage
    9124 · Car parking
    9130 · Travel and subsistence
    9132 · Hotels
    9134 · Subsistence
    9136 · Transportation
    9140 · Entertainment
    9150 · Training
    9160 · Staff refreshments
	Overheads are the business expenses incurred whilst operating that do not relate to the specific costs of the product or service described above. A large proportion will tend to relate to staff, not just their salary, but also their travel, subsistence and training as they go about their work.
	Note that entertainment is a good example of a business expense that is not tax deductible in the UK. Your accountant will be able to help you better understand these kinds of expenses, but you need to realise they will not reduce your tax bill.

Account code and description	Notes
9200 · EXPENSES 9210 · Office supplies 9215 · Marketing and advertising 9220 · Subscriptions and memberships 9225 · Telephone and broadband 9230 · Postage and delivery 9235 · IT and website services 9240 · Insurance 9245 · Accountancy 9250 · Professional fees 9255 · Office rent 9260 · Business rates 9275 · Utilities 9280 · Cleaning 9285 · Repairs and maintenance 9290 · Filing and compliance 9295 · Research and development	The exact categories of expenses that you choose will depend on your business activity, but this list gives a good range of what you are likely to need. More categories will help you understand where the money is being spent, but too many can be overkill. Some expenses may also qualify for special tax treatment, for example, R&D may be worth tracking because it can qualify for additional tax relief. These considerations are worth discussing through with your accountant based on the type of business you are running.
9300 · OTHER EXPENSES 9310 · Sundries 9320 · Corporation tax 9330 · Depreciation expense 9340 · Interest expense 9350 · Bank service charges 9360 · Bad debts 9370 · Other expenses	There are plenty of expenses that arise in just being in business; unfortunately there will be one-off expenses, taxes, fees, levies, charges and bad debts that you will also need to be aware of and try to reduce.

Table 11.2. An example chart of accounts and some of the considerations for each section.

Financial planning

Payroll is an important part of business finances. It often makes up a significant proportion of a company's fixed overheads, it has to be paid on time, and it often includes other mandatory payments such as tax, National Insurance (or equivalent) and pension contributions or levies. These often need to be paid at the same time to the government or other statutory bodies. Therefore, forecasting cashflow with regards to salary payments is crucial.

It is well worth noting which expenses are also not tax deductible (for example in the UK, entertainment can be charged as an expense to a company, but cannot be offset against tax). These are useful to know in predicting your tax bill which itself can have an impact on cashflow.

Tax is a complex area that requires the skills of a qualified accountant to advise you on, but there are a few fundamental things to watch from a cash flow perspective.

Understanding your projected profit before year end can also help you minimize your taxes. For example, in the UK you could make some additional pension contributions through salary sacrifice, or you could top up your employees' salaries with some performance bonuses so that you optimize your costs against any surplus. Equally, you may want to plan for a dividend payment, so ensuring you have sufficient profit and indeed cash to pay it in a timely manner.

You need to understand when a tax bill will come due; often it is a few months (nine, generally, in the case of the UK) after the company's year end. So a year ending on 31st March usually means tax is paid during December at the latest. This can have some bearing on selecting your tax year, as you may not want your tax bill to coincide with a busy time of the year (like Christmas) when you are needing good levels of cash reserves to finance production or sales. Equally, you may not want year end to be in the middle of a busy period or just ahead of a key period where you may have taken many down payments but not delivered the goods or services.

For example, if you are an event organizer with a flagship event every year, you probably do not want your year end to be too close in the calendar. In the case of an event company that I run, the annual event is early October, and year end is 31st March. It means most invoices relating to the forthcoming event can be raised after year end so they are in the year of the event which keeps things simpler from an accruals perspective, and any outstanding payments or receipts from the October event are easily cleared or chased before the end of the financial year. Furthermore, the period in April and May when the year's accounts are being prepared is also relatively quiet.

Another key consideration about cashflow and paying tax is that your tax bill may easily exceed the cash in the bank. It may seem counterintuitive in that cash in the bank ought to be there based on income minus expenses, and if all the expenses are largely tax deductible, there should not be much difference. Well, in theory yes, but there is an issue that comes with assets, workflow and stock in how they are treated by tax authorities.

Take assets; these are treated in specific ways by tax authorities and in the UK, for example, tangible equipment assets are in general set against an investment allowance in the first year, so they may be depreciated on your books over say three years, but charged in full as an expense in the first year from a tax perspective. This is fine in the first year, but can lead to surprises in later years when your accounts show depreciation expenses that are not tax deductible, so your corporation tax bill may be somewhat higher than anticipated.

There is no easy way for you, the entrepreneur, to foresee all these issues unless you are either a trained tax accountant or take a keen interest in the financial subtleties of your business. However, a good tactic is to talk with your accountant if there is a specific sizable investment that you need to make (such as equipment, plant, machinery or property improvements) so that you can predict the effect on your profit and tax. This will help with your cashflow management, and also highlight other ways to mitigate the tax bill such as schemes like the UK's R&D tax credits which may well apply.

Exit warrant

When you sign off your filing for each financial year, your records are expected to be accurate and honest. Investors and potential acquirers require the same, so be sure you understand the figures and have not cooked the books.

Similar complexities can arise if projects have been completed in a financial year but the customer has yet to pay you, or you have bought stock which is seen as a short-term asset that should not necessarily be expensed straight away, but rather held as a depreciating asset until it is sold or written off.

I have had experience with one company that provided a service and was paid upfront; ie, customers paid for the service and then the service was delivered by the company once the customer had themselves completed some tasks. This model generated a lot of cash, but the margins were actually quite slim because it was based around volumes. In such a case, the cashflow was relatively good, but it was easy to lose sight of liabilities; particularly as the supply of services was dependent on the customer getting prepared and coming back.

In such situations, it is tempting to spend the cash being generated on growth; such as recruiting more people and marketing, or on reward; such as increasing salaries and bonuses. But the key metric to understand is what the cost of the services really are and how much is left to pay for the overheads and further investment (spending).

Dividends are paid from your company's profit after tax. Any surplus not paid out as dividends is then classed as retained earnings. If your company remains profitable and not all is paid out in dividends, these retained earnings grow and so in general they create a cash reserve for future investment or indeed as a way to ease cashflow as the business grows. Therefore, it is not usually wise to pay out all the surplus as dividends, but it can be tax efficient at a personal level for the founder shareholders to take some. Again, talk to your accountant about this, as the rules have changed recently in the UK, and every jurisdiction will have their own regulations.

For a pre-revenue start-up, profits and dividends are things to aspire to, and cashflow is often easy to see but terrifying to manage. The only source of funds will be investments, grants or possibly loans. The burn rate (the rate at which cash is spent in the absence of significant sales) will determine the timeline until it runs out, and this needs to be carefully managed in terms of raising new investment or starting to generate sales. The principal objective is to have enough of a handle on the situation to see six or so months out when cash will become tight, because it will likely take that long to close a round of investment. In such situations, you do want a bit of leeway so that you are not in a poor negotiating position near the closure of an investment deal.

Staff expense forms

Other tools that will help you keep a grip on finances are some templates that you can add to the DN register. The first is a staff expense form. Even if it is just you making the initial claims as a director, you do need to make sure this is properly documented for tax compliance, as well as making it easier when it comes to end of year accounts.

Ideally you want the expense form to stipulate the account code that the expense relates to. This will help both the finance department and you keep tabs on costs, and generally speaking staff are only likely to claim a few things from the long list already discussed in Table 11.2. Typically, these will be:

- Car mileage

- Car parking

- Hotel accommodation

- Subsistence

- Transportation

- Entertainment

- Office supplies

If the company is VAT registered (or equivalent), the expense form also needs to capture any VAT component of a claim. And there is also a need to keep track of any foreign currency expenses and exchange rates. Finally, have in place a system that ensures the employee claiming the expense signs an original, which is approved by a manager or director, before being processed through the accounting software and paid. It is also good practice to have the bookkeeper or co-director approve any other director's expenses, so that oversight is evident.

Financial processes to smooth scale-up

Even if, as you start out, you are doing all the approval, verification and monitoring yourself, as you grow it will be easy to delegate the subtasks. This is important for tax compliance and also to ensure fraudulent claims are not made by employees; something you may consider unlikely but as the company grows, the opportunity for this to slip by increases too.

The finance department will also be responsible for other aspects of the business. One of these is maintaining the asset register as they will need to keep track of the value of assets for the balance sheet. As such, they could also be tasked with labelling the assets and having sight of them each year to ensure they are each still in the company.

It is also worth having a clear policy as to what constitutes a company asset. From an accounting perspective, it may be an item over say £100 in value. But there may also be lower value items that you want to label and track, like the staff logbooks the first of which we made a point of labelling MyCo-CC-AN0001.

If you are a technology start-up you are almost certainly looking for government grants to support your finances and fund some of the early product development. This is to be encouraged, but do make sure that you understand the timelines and limitations of the grants being sought.

Firstly, grants tend to take a lot of time and effort to bid for, so they may be a distraction if the chances of winning are relatively low. They also tend to be quite bureaucratic in that you will need to fill in numerous forms and provide further supporting evidence to claim the grant in stages.

It also brings along another issue which is that grants tend to be based on a reimbursement claim which means you already need to have sufficient cash to pay for things yourself before you will receive the money back, and sometimes this process can be long and drawn out.

Finally, grants tend to pay only a percentage value of all the qualifying expenses. Each grant will be different, but often it may be at a 40% or 60% level. What this means is that for every £1000 you spend on the project, you can only claim £400 or £600 from the grant. Furthermore, you can often only claim what you have spent in cash terms, so if you are an entrepreneur taking little or no salary, then you cannot claim you and your co-founders are worth £100,000 a year if you are only paying £10,000 to yourself in cash. You can of course decide to pay yourself more because of the grant, but then you have the 40% or 60% problem outlined above in which you will need to find extra cash in the business to have paid the balance.

For the SME it is also advisable to keep your corporate structure simple. It is galling that the large multinationals can set up complex offshore structures to reduce their tax liabilities, but as a start-up you are unlikely to have access to the costly expertise that will enable you to do this. Tempting though it may be to create a global holding company in the British Virgin Islands and an IP holding company in the Netherlands, and an EU trading HQ in Ireland, this complexity will create untold compliance costs for your fledgling company that probably far outweigh early tax savings even if they could be realised. Also, if the people who control these corporate entities all reside and operate from one country like the UK, it is likely the tax authorities will see it all as a UK company anyway. So, keep it simple.

Take-away and to-do list

- Whether you like the idea of monitoring finances or not, your business will live or die by how you well you keep track of them. Put some simple systems in place that you understand so that your valuable cash is not subject to wastage, fraud or mismanagement.

- ☐ Set up your accounting structure to clearly show different cost items.

- ☐ Create a monthly checklist to stay on top of the accounts and force a regular review of the financial statement.

12.

CORPORATE BRANDING AND
THE STYLE POLICE

Aiming for consistent branding

Nowadays, corporate image is becoming less and less tangible with the wide use of the internet and social media. Where your company is depicted in some written or graphical form, it is important to offer a coherent and consistent branding. This starts with your logo and includes your tag line, your typeface, and the layout and tone of the rest of your marketing collateral and material.

Company logo

Logos are surprisingly divisive things. Everyone has an opinion about them, thinking them too colourful, too old fashioned, too plain and so on. We once had an angel investor who was determined to change our logo once he had made an investment in our start-up. There were so many other things to do, and the logo may not have been the best in the world, but it did have relevance and it was already widely in use. In the end, we did change the logo, mainly to appease the value-adding investor in question. This activity required a huge amount of distracting work, as we had to change the website and the stationery (letterheads, business cards etc), as well as packaging and product labels. Ironically, we went on to sell the business before we had got far with this rebranding exercise, then the company name changed within the new corporate family and we actually had yet another company logo to roll out.

By all means, use a designer to create your logo, but if you plan to do it yourself, create something that looks professional and ensure you end up with one final master version as your source file, not a host of variations. Also, make sure the logo is original and that it can be readily understood in both colour and black-and-white forms.

Invaluable capex

Your logo is an important company asset, so it is well worth doing it properly from the start. You can save spending money with an expensive design agency by using online logo design crowdsourcing services such as Fiverr. £5-£500 depending on who you engage

---

Keep the source file in which the graphic was drawn and create a series of files for that logo in different sizes and ideally as a colour, grey scale and black and white version. Keep these files in vector, png and jpg file formats, for example, named as CompanyLogo100px etc, so that you have a range of sizes: 100 pixels, 250 pixels and 500 pixels in width to suit a variety of situations. Save them to the 00-DOCS shared folder where those that you want to have access to them can without bothering you.

A design guide

Along with the logo, you should also create what the industry refers to as a brand manual or design guide. Professional firms will almost certainly do this for you, but it can be done quite simply yourself. This design guide shows the logo in various forms for use on dark and light backgrounds, along with stipulations about the clear area (margin) to be left around it, as well as any details about colour pallet and accompanying font for any branded company material. The document also clarifies any tag lines to be used by the company with the logo, and other layout standards that are to be applied to marketing collateral. The guide can also extend to product logos and other related logos such as 'authorized reseller' logos. The brand manual will often contain examples of how *not* to use a logo; for example, repeated in tiles, too close to another or with associated text in the wrong position. Often the brand manual is itself a work of art, created by the graphic design company and embodying your company's brand in terms of tone, layout and presentation.

The brand manual will also help you think about certain formats for the logo; for example, an elongated logo (perhaps because of the company name) can be a problem when the width is limited. Therefore, you may wish to create a square variant of your logo or name; for example, to be used as an icon in some web applications like Twitter, Instagram or LinkedIn.

Once again, keep a record of the official versions of the files so they are readily available; for example, CompanyLogoSquare100px for the 100-pixel-wide square variant. These versions should be added to your brand manual with clear guidelines as to when they are used instead of the main logo.

Company stationery

Once you have your logo, you will want to create business cards, letterheads, compliments slips and other company documents. These will need your logo, tag line (if any), postal address, web address and contact details (such as phone, mobile phone, email etc), all set out in a consistent manner. Ensure your controlled company information document is used as the source of all the printed details that appear on the stationery.

The marketing collateral also needs to use the same typeface (font) and style in terms of heading, capitalization, terminology (eg, Tel, Phone, Landline, ☎). You can add these guidelines (or requisites) to your brand manual.

Once you have settled on the design for each document, save them as a template in the usual DN number format, so that others can use them rather than creating their own variants with different styles. Where letterheads and business cards need different names added, these can be saved as MyCo-CC-DN01234.1a or b to indicate variants of the same version. If in the future you move office, for example, all of the variants will be updated, and you will have all the subsets to hand on which to make the changes. Of course, the brand manual itself will also be saved and available as a controlled document with a DN number.

Web presence

Your website is also a key marketing resource that needs to make use of the logo and overall branding. As such, it should have the right typeface, colours, contact details and tone to fit with your branding. So the brand manual could also provide guidance here; such as the heading logo and relative size so that your website headings match with headings in other printed documents.

Your website is also likely to have some resources for customers, such as white papers, specification sheets, instruction manuals etc. These should also be created in the house style, using the right logo and font, so that each looks professional and consistent. Public documents like specification sheets that can change in time should also make use of the DN system so that you know which version people are referring to and if something is superseded in the future.

Unfortunately, there is more to a website than how it looks. Ideally, the marketing department needs to stay on top of it in terms of functionality and usability. For example, in the couple of years that I have been writing this book, websites have had to become mobile friendly often using responsive frameworks so that they can adapt to desktop, tablet and mobile phone screens of different sizes. Each of these formats also needs to be checked that they are readable on example devices around the office.

Websites also need to undergo search engine optimization (SEO) so that they appear near the top of key relevant online searches. This can be a moving target because Google, Bing and Yahoo all change their criteria over time. In the end, you probably want to make sure that keywords and other meta data fields are complete and relate to the text and business. You can do text searches yourself, but they will be influenced by where you are located and whether you are in fact logged in to the service and have a profile that also affects the results.

Finally, there are technical issues to consider with your website as well. Presently, Google is starting to rank websites higher that offer a security certificate (appear as https:// rather than http://). This is another thing to sort out and maintain, but also imperative if you are collecting any login or user data through your website service.

Policing your brand

In time, the marketing department will be responsible for ensuring that your branding is used consistently throughout. Until you have a department, this is likely to be up to you the founding directors. Some people find this easier to do than others; not everyone is artistic and can be bothered to enforce the rules, but as a company that is growing, it really is important to project a consistent image and to police it so that everyone uses the same style. It will be a lot easier to maintain and update documents if this is the case too, and customers will almost certainly notice the broad consistency and believe they are dealing with an organized company.

As you grow more, so policing your brand will become even more difficult. It is hard enough to ensure that your staff all use it properly, but larger companies also need to ensure agents and overseas companies follow the rules as well. This is certainly easier to do if you put in place guidelines early on and make it straightforward for your employees to find the right templates.

Exit warrant

As your identity, your company brand is a valuable asset. It may well be what attracted an investor or acquirer to find out more about you in the first place. Therefore, make sure it is correctly protected, used and monitored in all the sectors in which you operate and that you do indeed have the rights to use it as a company. When you sell your business, the new owners may change it all, but foremost they may be buying the brand.

In Singular ID, we won a business-plan competition that enabled us to set up a business overseas from Singapore in northern Italy. We had to consider how the branding was to be applied; was the company to be a simple subsidiary for the country or indeed the region (Europe) and was it going to focus on specific relevant markets (like luxury goods) or tackle everything.

Not all of these considerations are marketing issues, but ensuring the logo, letterheads, business cards, Italian language marketing collateral and so forth are consistent most certainly was a marketing issue, and the overall strategy needed to be clear to feed in to the marketing activity.

In the end, the subsidiary was marketed as Singular ID Italia, and the country logo tweaked to reflect this. It was decided to focus on Italy first, across all sectors as appropriate, and see if other European business followed.

Take-away and to-do list

- You will want your company to project a consistent and professional brand image in every way it operates. This involves putting in place some templates and policies so that your company is presented in the right manner in a broad range of media from printed form to online digital form, in its marketing literature and how its products and services look and feel.

☐ Design or source a logo and create a series of versions in various sizes and formats.

☐ Agree on fonts, colours and formatting options for your brand and document in a brand manual.

☐ Ensure your website is mobile friendly, has some level of search engine optimization and ideally is https://.

13.

PUBLICITY, SMOKE AND MIRRORS

Keep the news flowing

There is a fine, but important, line between strong marketing and lying. It is crucial to always tell the truth in business, whether that is in terms of how well a technology works, what a product can do, what you can deliver as a service or how your company is performing when you talk to investors.

However, equally you must enthuse and impress. You must show that your business is growing or has the potential to do so, that your product is a must-have, and that your future as an enterprise is bright. There is an art to this, but coming across as intelligent and knowledgeable helps. You have to be living and breathing your business and fully appreciate the competitive landscape and technological hurdles.

Exit warrant

Unlike the trend of fake news that is sweeping the globe at the moment, you need to make sure the stories you spin are truthful, as suitors will read them and may well have been drawn to you through them.

We used to face this problem routinely with Singular ID because our high technology anti-counterfeiting system was pretty advanced and when it was explained to people, they seemed to think it was invincible. We were always at pains to say that our solution provided security tags that were 'prohibitively difficult to copy'. This was very different to saying that our tags were 'impossible to copy' as you never know how much effort someone might put in to disprove your point. So be careful about saying your product is infallible, completely secure or unbreakable, for example.

Marketing your business is not just about selling to a prospective customer. It is about attracting talented future employees, convincing investors to become stakeholders and enthusing suppliers and would-be collaborators to get on board and be part of the success story.

Growing a contact list

It is well worth creating a mailing list of contacts that you would like to keep updated. Name, email address and some kind of category is quite useful, because you'll be able to use the category later to help filter and hone the mailing list for different types of news as the company grows. A Microsoft Excel sheet or equivalent Google Sheet is more than sufficient as a start, but you could get ahead by subscribing to an emailing service such as Mailchimp or Constant Contact. Some of these services are free for low volume usage so you should not need any financial outlay to get started. Table 13.1 summarizes some key information to make up your mailing list.

Contact details	Name, email, address, phone number
Status	Subscribed, unsubscribed
Category	Staff, customer, press, collaborator, supplier, investor
Receive	Press releases, newsletter, offers

Table 13.1 Useful information for a contact mailing list.

The marketing mailing list needs to be kept separate from your own personal or general work mailing lists, because in the future this list will be further developed by your marketing team or PR agency.

Typical contacts at the start might be friends and family who are taking an interest in your venture, potential investors you are talking with, and business contacts you are starting to build relationships with perhaps in organizations like the local chamber of commerce. Add a reporter or editor from your local newspaper too. Typical categories would be friend (relative, friend, ex-colleague), supplier (strategic supplier such as landlord, accountant, collaborator, legal counsel), investor (business angel, venture capitalist, bank manager), press contact (newspaper editor, journalist, trade journal editor), and customer (potential or actual).

Expanding your mailing list is also crucial so that you extend the reach of your marketing in the future. Once you have started your list of contacts, you and your staff need to add to it as you meet new people whilst networking. Add names of those attending your own events, and create a simple form on your website for people to sign up to get more news. Services like Mailchimp can create an integrated sign-up page that can be linked from your website or emails, automatically adding submissions to your list. Usually a name and email address is sufficient, but if you can get a little more information, that can be valuable too; such as where they heard about you, if they are already a customer.

Try to have one master list as this will also help you manage those whom might unsubscribe in the future. That way you will automatically honour their request and not keep emailing them news when they have asked not to hear from you again.

It is also important to put in place a simple process for your staff to add to the database. Firstly, you probably want HR to add your employees, as there is nothing worse for your colleagues to hear news about your company after people outside have. If they receive the same press release, they will be informed, so will be able to respond appropriately if their business contacts mention it. The sales, marketing and BD teams also need to have their contacts added as a matter of course. Today employees can make use of services like LinkedIn to grow their contact base. Personal social networking may well benefit you as a company too, although the connections will be lost if and when and the employee leaves.

Finally, you need to consider privacy and security. At this point, you need to be aware that it is no longer acceptable to collect data from members of the public for the sake of it. You need to ensure they are aware how you will use the data (for example, to keep them informed about company or product news) and you need to ensure the data is secure and not shared or leaked with others. This is actually a minefield to navigate and in complicated situations you may need legal advice, especially as new privacy and data laws are coming into force, particularly, in Europe through the General Data Protection Regulation. In the UK, it is well worth registering with the Information Commissioners Office early on, as for a modest fee this will help you stay compliant and highlight some of the issues to think about as you complete the registration form.

Press releases

Sending out regular but interesting press releases can really help build the buzz around your business. If you achieve a significant milestone such as signing up a first major customer, securing investment, winning a competition, having a visit from your local MP and so on, then put together a simple press release and send it out. Obviously, you need to ensure that any details are agreeable to any other party mentioned or quoted, but having a third party highlighted in this way adds credence to the news.

Create a press release template that can be used each time as the basis. Usually press releases will comprise a short snappy title, a slightly longer explanatory subtitle, the date and city of release, and then a series of paragraphs outlining the story. Add some quotations from yourself or appropriate parties (making sure they have agreed to what is being said and in what context). At the end, add a paragraph about your company and any other organization referred to in the press release (for example the investor or customer). This editorial content can be used by the journalist to create a more informed story. Finally, ensure there is a web address, contact name (probably yours), phone number (probably your business mobile number or your office number) and an email (probably your email or the generic department email marketing@yourcompany.com). Bear in mind that all this information is going to be in the public domain, so do not mention anything confidential, sensitive, untrue or something you would rather not tell people about like your personal phone number or home address.

If you have relevant photographs, include these with captions at the end and either send high-resolution ones to reporters or ensure they know that they can be quickly made available. Images are often valuable in catching attention, improving the chances of your story appearing in a newspaper, trade journal or magazine.

Invaluable capex

Every now and again it is good to buy something frivolous for your company that lightens the mood, boosts productivity in a light-hearted way or simply makes you chuckle. It could be a table tennis kit, bean bags or lava lamp. If the title of this chapter resonated with you, why not buy a disco ball and smoke machine for the office for days when your publicity works well. Cost: £25.

If you use plain email to circulate your press release or newsletter, make sure you blind copy (bcc) all your addressees for two reasons. One, these are your prized contacts, so do not let others know who they are. Two, nobody likes their email address shared with a large group of others without their permission. In this case, also send the press release as a pdf as it keeps it self-contained and is harder to edit than in a Word document format. Importantly, the journalist will still be able to cut and paste the text to build up their piece.

If you use one of the email services, keep the layout simple for a press release, as news desk editors and journalists will want to extract the main text into their own software so that they can write a piece. Keeping this process straightforward for them increases the chances of publication.

Newsletters and e-bulletins

General newsletters are also useful for keeping interested parties up to speed with developments. It all depends on your business, as sometimes newsletters will be crucial to keep customers engaged. If you are an early-stage technology business yet to sell a product, a newsletter is still beneficial. Keeping the news flowing will mean that future customers, future partners and future investors are already knowledgeable of your progress and may be secretly hoping to be part of your success story.

For a bulletin or newsletter, usually sent electronically, design a template around the branding of your company so that your corporate image is consistent. As discussed above, use a service like Mailchimp, as this will help you to catalogue previous issues, pull up the template or last issue to save time for the new one and allow you to keep track of the data around each bulletin or campaign. These kinds of services are also ideal because they make sure recipients are all sent a blind copy and your own mail server does not inadvertently become blacklisted as a source of spam because of the volume of email traffic sent in one go.

Ideally, you will set up the account as part of the marketing department, so use something like the generic email, 'marketing@ yourcompany.com', as the username for the account. Once you hire a marketing manager, they can take control of this account straight away. You can always add another username such as yours or 'ceo@ yourcompany.com' or 'md@yourcompany.com' to maintain access and overall control.

Clippings and alerts

A few decades ago, organizations would subscribe to a press-clipping service to receive summaries of where they had appeared in the news. This enabled the marketing department to keep any eye on campaigns and how well a press release was received and used. Today, there are free services like Google alerts. At the very least you should sign up, and so should your marketing department, to receive alerts on your company name, product name or key market sector name. You will be kept informed of when your company is cited or something significant happens in the market place. You may also want to monitor your competitors in this way too.

I once had an example where a work experience student mentioned our company name on a social media post in the early days of social networking. It was not too bad, but taken out of context, it was not great. It was something about being a bit bored on Friday afternoon and wanting to leave for the weekend. At the time, because social media was a new phenomenon, such posts stood out if someone searched on the company. Therefore, having had an alert I was able to discuss it with the student and suggest that the post was taken down as inappropriate.

Today, it is much more difficult to police in this way, as the sheer volume of social media traffic means your employees and company could be referenced quite widely. Now it is a case of keeping an eye on it and responding quickly to any customer complaints through these channels.

Spreading the word

Getting positive free publicity is a great way to propel your business, as it reinforces your leadership position in the market if you are seen to be an organization that the press refers to. Newspapers and magazines are always on the lookout for interesting newsworthy articles, as although they may get their revenue from advertising, they are reliant on good quality content.

Your aim should therefore be to help them with prize copy. Create a list of local papers, trade journals, even national papers that might be interested in your news. Consider this from the angle of not just your products or services, but also your success stories or operations (for example, news that you have won project grant funding, filed a novel patent, won a prize or raised finance). Local chambers of commerce and other business organizations will even like to hear about your latest recruit and their background, and this can provide great publicity because it shows your business is growing and is a good excuse to let readers know what you do and where you are based.

Another tactic is to become a thought leader for the industry you are involved in. This is particularly useful for niche and technology businesses where experts may be few and far between, and reporters would like to refer to one to expand on a story. You can establish yourself as an industry leader by blogging or writing white papers on the subject, and letting local reporters or press agencies know about your knowledge. The result could be interviews on the radio or television in which your company name may get a mention in passing.

Taking part in conferences can also be a good way to publicize your business. Not all conferences need you to pay for the privilege, and I tend to avoid at all costs conferences that expect you as the speaker to pay. It is also possible to speak at events that are not closely related to your business sector, but can still provide valuable exposure. I was once invited to speak at a conference about inward investment and how cities and countries can entice new businesses; my experience with starting and growing a new venture as a foreigner in Singapore was the hook, and at the time I was still in the thick of it as the CEO. The conference organizers paid my travel expenses to Europe and I had a fantastic opportunity to explain what we were doing to an audience of influential people whom I would otherwise have been unlikely to have met.

Press cuttings on file

As you generate publicity, it is a good idea to keep a file of hard copy press cuttings. These can be a great record for the future when you are looking to sell your business, as it will show how you have been recognized by others in the big wide world. It will also enable you to make copies for the noticeboard, front desk or reception area coffee table. That way, employees and visitors will also see your publicity and this has a really positive impact on how they perceive your business. When investors drop in, they will also pick up on the vibe and want to be part of the success story.

Sometimes you need to run publicity campaigns that are a little different to stimulate interest. These can grab the attention of journalists, or they could even go viral and reach many potential customers quickly. As the organizer of the Malvern Festival of Innovation, I face the problem that the festival ought to practice what it preaches and be creative in how it markets itself. I have not got the full answer to this yet, but I do try to do something a little different each year to attract attention.

For example, one year I was able to persuade the train company First Great Western (now GWR) to name their early morning service out of London Paddington to Great Malvern 'The Innovation Express'. This involved some carriage window stickers and people did indeed notice them and mentioned their observations on social media. In a later year, we were able to get another train company, London Midland, operating from Birmingham to call their services the 'Innovation Shuttles' and add this name to the customer information screens. Then we did some colourful adhesive pavement stickers for around town to join up the venues and published a London Underground style map to show the routes which we dubbed the 'Innovation Get-around'. These initiatives, with colourful flags in the high street during the lead up to the event, made people aware of the festival and made them think it was bigger and more established than it probably was, because it was being supported in unconventional ways.

Finally, we also ran an April fool news item one year that claimed the Malvern Hills had just been planted with genetically modified grasses coloured in the shades of our logo. These would reach their peak intensity mid-autumn to coincide with the event and thus provide a spectacular backdrop to the festival. I think 1st April is the only exception for a fake business news story.

Take-away and to-do list

- Good news stories can generate a lot of great publicity for your business, and with a bit of thought you should be able to get regular free publicity by helping journalists and reporters with their content. As your business grows, so should your mailing list so that you can keep contacts updated with your progress and let them share in the buzz.

☐ Create and maintain a company contact mailing list for news and publicity.

☐ Produce a press release and newsletter template in your style according to your brand manual.

14.

SOCIAL MEDIA, DAILY TEDIA?

The rise of social media

Something that businesses did not have to contend with ten years ago was social networking and the immediacy of this marketing channel. Previously businesses could create a website, issue a press release and dampen down any bad news that may appear in a letters' column. Today, it happens at a push of a button prefixed by a hashtag or an @ symbol.

During my time working on the start-up in Singapore, Facebook emerged as a new personal tool to hook up with old friends, LinkedIn arrived as a new way to show off your CV, and Twitter started a little later largely in the domain of personal users. So, we did not really have to worry much about social media because it was just starting in itself. In many ways, we had a lucky escape because on reflection I am not sure we would have had the time nor bandwidth to stay on top of it all as well. Now, however, you have even more balls to juggle.

The primary issue for business owners and their teams is harnessing this force and staying with it for the course in a consistent and timely manner.

Firstly, a company Twitter feed that has been going for two years, but last uttered a word of wisdom six months ago does not fill a prospective customer, nor indeed an investor, with confidence that the enterprise is still in business. Equally, a feed of irrelevant drivel is not going to send the right message either.

Social networking is now a requirement for marketing and a means of engaging with your customer, and there are few business situations where you can lie low and not participate. Unfortunately, the growing number of channels (Facebook, LinkedIn, Twitter, Google+, Instagram, Pinterest, YouTube, WhatsApp, SnapChat, to name but a few) means that you need to understand the workings of each of them, create multiple accounts, establish cross-platform consistency, and then keep them all updated and vibrant.

Each platform has its own etiquette and approach. LinkedIn is a professional platform inextricably linked to you or your employee's own resume. Twitter a concise stream where your intellect will be measured by the sophistication of your sound bite. Facebook a more informal bulletin board likely to be interrogated by friends or customers in their leisure time. And so it goes on: you will be marked on the quality of your content, the relevance of your message, and the timeliness of your comments. Your company's brand can be enhanced, diminished or damaged beyond recognition by careless use.

As such, you will want to establish your feed early on. Keep the flow of comment and content steady and regular, but do not overdo it. You will only build a rod for your own back. Think what you hope to achieve from each platform and consider carefully whether your business needs to be on them all.

Effective social media processes

I believe that the first golden rule in social media is to separate personal life from business. There are some instances where your personal account can be used to enhance your business if for example you have built a sizable following. However, generally it is better to build a social media following in any given account directly attributable to your business. This is because these people are likely to be genuinely interested in the products or services you offer. Also, when you come to exit the business, the social media accounts can all legitimately form part of the intangible value of the business and be sold with the company. This adds value to the business and means the acquirer can continue where you leave off. If it is your own personal account, you may have to cut the umbilical cord and start again. Your name on the account will not exactly go with the ongoing business if you are not at the helm.

Exit warrant

Make sure the social media accounts are registered to and controlled by the company, even if you outsource some of the activity, because investors and acquirers will want the value to reside within the business.

At the beginning, you will probably be doing the tweets and posts yourself, but over time you will want to delegate this activity to your marketing department. Hence, having a generic account username or email helps with this transition; so sign up initially to the services using, for example, the marketing@yourcompany.com email address.

It is then also possible to add other staff users to many accounts (like Google pages, Facebook groups and so on). The issue then is to keep track of who has access to what, as, if an employee leaves, you will need to revoke their access quickly. As your business starts using a multitude of online services, it can become tricky to manage. In the end, it is probably best to use a simple shared spreadsheet or database in the HR department to keep track of staff users. That way, when someone leaves there is a mechanism to cease their involvement with your social media stream.

Another issue with social networking is that over time the marketing department will want to spread their reach and start new accounts with new services. This is fine, but the brand needs managing and access to these new accounts need to be controlled. Usernames cannot be tied to the incumbent individual because all these outlets become valuable business assets. With this in mind, the policy should be that these accounts are opened by using the generic department usernames or emails. Further administrator rights should also be conferred on another manager or director.

Occasionally social media accounts get hacked, so be sure they are well protected with different passwords and that you have a second way to get back in to them registered with the service provider (like a mobile phone number). The process also needs to ensure these details are recorded internally and maintained up to date. A hacked account could start sending out embarrassing messages and will need to be reclaimed as quickly as possible.

Multiple accounts can be managed using something like TweetDeck or Hoot Suite. These platforms allow several social networking channels to be controlled from one dashboard, and they also enable multiple users to access and post to the social network services.

An extension to your brand

It is also essential that the various channels are consistent across the board in terms of branding and style. So, the Twitter profile graphic, the Twitter header backdrop, the Facebook profile graphic, the Facebook header backdrop and so on should all be equivalent and derived from the logo file and company website graphics previously created.

You will also need to ensure the profile information is correct and consistent on all platforms. This includes the company address, contact details, opening and closing times, and so on. I find that it is often worth keeping the details on the various social media pages to a minimum and pointing clearly to your company website for the seminal information. This way, you will have fewer platforms to update as things change and in turn you will drive traffic to your main site.

Social media is all about content, and so you will want to ensure that the company regularly provides comment that is engaging and consistent with the brand ethos. It is also imperative that posts stay on message and do not deviate to complain about a late train or something political (unless this is linked to your business). It is easy to alienate potential customers or suppliers by posting something that could be interpreted the wrong way or goes against the opinion of the recipient. Equally, it is important to ensure nothing libelous, confidential or commercially sensitive is posted, as this could result in costly litigation with no easy way to undo what has been published. Potential investors and acquirers will probably review all of your social media feeds to check for problems, so keep this in mind as well.

Whoever posts to the company's social media needs to be properly trained and understand the public-facing nature of the job. Equally, the person responsible for social media needs to be able to post items without going through hoops for clearance, as the last thing you want is for you or another senior staff member to be spending time approving tweets that are probably only topical if sent quickly.

Measuring impact

There is also a benefit to understanding why your business is active in the social networking ecosystem. Firstly, an aim is almost certainly to attract more followers and this requires the account itself to follow others, monitor who is or is not following back, and be interactive with retweets (in the case of Twitter) and likes, shares and so forth (with Facebook for example). This can be a time-consuming activity in itself, but there is also a need to be responsive, as customers may use these channels to complain or seek advice.

If a social media response is slow, or a post is ignored, this does not go down well with the customer or prospect. Some services, such as Facebook, also monitor how quick an enquiry is answered and they rate the customer service aspect of your page openly as a result. So, you need to be monitoring all of this within your business and have staff to cover other staff in times of holiday or illness. An out-of-office email response is no longer sufficient; you need an away-from-social-media process too.

Despite all the activity, you will still probably have little understanding of the impact social media is really having on the business. Ultimately, you need to ask whether all the effort generates more sales or drives more traffic to your website? This can be very hard to deduce, so it is well worth putting a basic monitoring process in place.

Some key metrics to track, and discuss regularly as a marketing team say on a monthly basis are the number of posts, number of followers and level of interaction (retweets, replies, likes etc). This can also be augmented with some website analytics as to how many referrals to your webpage came from the various social media services. If you are an e-commerce business, then it should be relatively easy to link social media posts with sales as you can look for referrals to your online shop page that were both referred from a service like Twitter and resulted in a purchase. Moreover, you will be able to put a value on the referrals and see how this compares with the cost of running the social media channel.

Invaluable capex

Much of social media is free, although you can pay to promote posts. However, there are a few really low-cost mobile apps that allow you to track statistics relating to you accounts; for example, who has unfollowed you or is not following you back. These can be really helpful for your marketing activity, so worth spending a few pence trying some out. Twitfollow is one example. Outlay: 79p upwards on the Apple app store or Android play store.

Over time, your aim should be to understand what generates more quality followers, what leads to website referrals, what leads to sales and which channels are the most lucrative or least costly to manage. This will allow your team to optimize their social media activity for the benefit of the business. You should also benchmark against your competition; how do they use social media, how many followers do they have, what is their engagement like from post to post?

We did this kind of exercise recently for the Malvern Festival of Innovation. We paid a monthly fee to a local PR agency to tweet during the three months running up to the event. We monitored the quality of the tweets (in terms of being on message and generating retweets), the growth in followers, the regularity of tweets and responses (such as liking or retweeting a mention) and most importantly we looked at how may referrals to our website were generated. This analysis enabled us to put a direct cost to each referral and the result was sobering, because although the specific social media activity was certainly much higher than we could have managed internally, the actual cost of this exercise per successful outcome measured was higher than expected and certainly it was arguable as to whether it was worth the expense.

Take-away and to-do list

- Social media is a necessary evil, but chose which channels you will focus on and be prepared to post interesting, insightful and relevant content from this day forward. Review its impact regularly and work out what the cost benefit ratio is, ideally in monetary terms.

- ☐ Set up one or more social media accounts with the correct branding and user information.

- ☐ Create a process of regularly analyzing trends and data relating to each channel.

15.

STAFF MANAGEMENT: HERDING CATS, AVOIDING SCRATCHES

An expanding business needs to recruit good quality staff. Often it is a task overlooked or rushed in the whirlwind of growth. People can make or break a business, and in today's competitive global job market, it can be difficult to find and attract the right skills. As a start-up, you may also be perceived as a risky career move, so it will be equally important for you and the company to come across well in the interview, as it will be for the candidate to do so for you.

Recruiting staff

Putting in place a robust recruitment process early pays dividends, because employment law is complicated and employing people can be expensive and is highly regulated. There will be minimum wage levels, taxes, social security levies and other hidden costs to consider, many of which need to be paid on time and in full. Staff are also difficult to dismiss or lay off. Often, notice periods, lengths of service and holiday entitlements bring hidden yet accruing liabilities. Furthermore, sick pay, pensions, parental leave and so forth present further unknowns to the business.

With recruitment, make sure that you advertise the position as widely as possible (even if that is by low cost or free avenues like using social media, posting on job boards and publicizing through local community groups) so you attract several candidates and can create a shortlist. Make sure that your advert has a job specification that outlines the responsibilities and scope of the position; both so you know what you are really looking for and the right candidates will apply. When you receive an application, look at the quality of the covering letter and CV, both in terms of content, but also in terms of presentation and accuracy. It should be obvious that any spelling mistakes or poor grammar in documents of such importance to the applicant will re-occur more frequently when they start working for you.

I recommend that you keep detailed records of the selection process, because even as a small company you need to judge candidates on their merit. It is important you do not discriminate, because it is unlawful, leading to disputes that are costly and distracting for your business. Try to interview more than one person for a position so that you have comparisons. In the interview, involve other members of staff to seek a second (or third) opinion, as this will result in buy-in from within the company and colleagues may notice traits you have missed.

It is also good practice to have an interview template in your DN repository for staff to use and complete, both to guide the interview but also to report their thoughts afterwards. If you interview several candidates over a period of time, a set of notes like this can be invaluable in making an informed decision. An example is given in Table 15.1

Interview category	Aspects to query and record
Job description activities	Past relevant experience
	Examples of activities
Qualifications	Levels and suitability
	Which aspects help with tasks
	Numeracy and language skills
Personality	Evidence of self-management
	Evidence of teamwork
	Confidence and attitude
	Examples of success in past
	Examples of difficult tasks
Expectation	Salary, hours and holiday pay
	Career path and five-year plan
	Other benefits
	Reasons for application

Table 15.1. Examples of notes to keep in an interview during recruitment.

Keep all the applicants' details securely on file so that you have the original information for your recruits, but also a pool of potential candidates to contact in the future should another vacancy arise or the first choice falls through.

Finally, as part of the recruitment process, seek references from past employers or their school or college. Then be clear on the job offer and any period of probation. It might seem obvious, but many start-ups simply do not go to the effort of dotting the i's and crossing the t's when it comes to taking on new staff. The cost of doing it wrong could easily equate to several months of the new recruit's salary and then the added cost of going back through the recruitment process again.

Inducting new arrivals

When a new member of staff comes on board, take them through a documented staff-induction process. Create a checklist to complete using a controlled document in the DN system, and have both the inductor and inductee sign the completed sheet.

Table 15.2 gives an example checklist. It could be a paper copy that gets circulated with the new recruit to be signed at each point before being filed back with HR. Or you could have an online checklist that you log in via an app or through some specialist ERP or HR management software on the intranet or in the cloud.

DEP HR

Given by: _____ Signed by staff: _____

Name: _____ Mobile: _____

Home: _____

Address: _____

_____

Next of kin: _____

Mobile: _____

☐ Copy of passport, driving license or official ID obtained

☐ Staff handbook provided (MyCo-CC-DNxxxx. ☐)

☐ Other policies explained (MyCo-CC-DNxxxx. ☐)

☐ Confidentiality agreement signed (MyCo-CC-DNxxxx. ☐)

☐ Lab / log book issued (MyCo-CC-AN_____)

☐ Add email to mailing list

☐ Phone directory updated

☐ Car details for car-parking: Make: _____ Model: _____ Colour: _____ Reg: _____

DEP FIN

Given by: _____ Signed by staff: _____

☐ P45 or other payroll documentation

☐ Bank details

DEP OPS / IT

Given by: _____ Signed by staff: _____

☐ Office / Desk location: _____

☐ keys provided

☐ Office roll-call list updated

☐ Wifi details / wireless key provided

☐ Web-portal username issued

☐ Shared calendars set up

Table 15.2. Example induction checklist.

As part of the process, you will need to see and probably keep copies of supporting documents (for example, an identification document like a passport, work permit where applicable, academic or professional certificates, driving licence, as well as documents relating to past employment and tax; the P45 in the UK).

Members of staff should have all their documents securely filed

151

in the HR department, including signed contracts, their pay slips, a holiday record form, timesheets and so forth.

The new member of staff will also read and understand various policies (like health and safety, use of computers, office security and so forth). These should be standalone documents in the DN document system or collated in a staff handbook which itself would have a DN designation. Note how the example checklist in Table 15.2 also captures the version numbers of the documents read so that staff can be given new versions to read when they are updated.

A structured induction is also an opportunity for departments other than HR to record certain tasks as well: for example, the marketing department to order business cards, IT to issue email and server login accounts, and facilities (or operations) to issue keys to the building and the desk, and that other forms like confidentiality agreements and intellectual property agreements are executed as appropriate.

Of course, in a start-up these steps may all be performed by the same person, but done from this virtual department perspective will mean it is easy for the departments to take on these responsibilities specifically as the company grows.

Exit warrant

Ensure your staff contracts are signed and on file so that the company's liability in terms of pay and service is clear and well documented. Potential investors and acquirers will want to see that staff are happy and they will need to be made aware of any past disagreements or tribunals.

Growing teams

As your company grows, so too the number of people within your organization, as well as the number of suppliers and customers with whom you all have to interact.

One of the key issues in a growing business is maintaining good levels of communication. Initially, the small group of up to ten or twenty people is generally manageable, unless some of the group are travelling extensively or based overseas. Once you start to grow beyond 20, tensions can mount because you will almost certainly need a more defined hierarchy of manager and subordinate, however passionate you are about a flat structure.

Problems arise when employees that were part of the original smaller team start to become detached from the decision-making process because of newly recruited middle managers or new team leaders. They once had a direct line to you or other founding directors, so were by default kept updated with the business developments and plans, even if it was just through unavoidable eavesdropping in the small shared office. As the company grows, they will possibly find themselves reporting to a newly recruited manager who filters information and acts as a barrier to the directors. As a result, they may feel left out of the business and sidelined. This situation will need managing.

These problems can create some significant growing pains, mainly because humans are complicated animals requiring emotional feedback and constant management. You will want to employ creative individuals with flair and drive, but this brings with it the need to provide some level of control.

Small companies work well because everyone can keep up to date, feel part of the team and there is little room for politics and dissent. As you grow beyond about a dozen people, the dynamic changes, and different camps will start to form. As you grow further, middle managers are required to help coordinate the functions and more time will be spent in meetings finding out what is going in and getting the facts collated. It becomes like steering a large ship, as changes in direction or strategy will take time to filter through the organization and be implememented. If different groups adopt changes at different rates this can confuse the business. And hidden ('skunk') projects tend to proliferate. These are lines of enquiry that continue to be pursued behind the scenes that may not fit with the new strategy, diverting effort and diluting results.

These problems can be pre-empted to some extent by having controls in place early on. Information can be pre-organized within departments in the company to make information sharing easier as the company grows, and this will allow new recruits with certain job functions to get up to speed quickly and feel part of the team without having to dig around for historic information. As such, a new recruit would be given the file access permissions associated with their department and job role, and they would be able to start useful work on day one with company templates, documents and general information automatically made available to them.

Communication can be maintained by ensuring an updated emailing list is maintained by HR that can be used easily by you and others in the company.

Appraising staff performance

Even in a hectic start-up business, it is necessary to set time aside on a regular basis to undertake formal reviews of staff performance. They could be quarterly, half yearly or annually, although half yearly is often a good time frame. By being formal, it is an opportunity to engage with staff and document from both sides what is going well and where there are areas for improvement. If there is poor performance, having regular meetings and records will help you to dismiss a member of staff lawfully should that unfortunately become necessary. Otherwise, you could be looking at a costly and distracting employment tribunal for unfair dismissal. Table 15.3 provides an example record sheet for such an exercise.

Name:	Position:
Appraisal date and time:	Appraiser:
Period covered:	
Time in present position:	Length of service:

Part A Appraisee to complete before the interview and return to the appraiser.

A1. State your understanding of your main duties and responsibilities

A2. Has this period been good/bad/satisfactory or otherwise for you; and why?

A3. What do you consider to be your most important achievements during this period?

A4. What do you like about working for MyCo?

A5. What do you dislike about working for MyCo?

A6. What elements of your job interest you the most?

A7. What elements of your job interest you the least?

A8. What elements of your job do you find easiest?

A9. What elements of your job do you find the most difficult?

A10. What do you consider to be your most important aims and tasks in the next year?

A11. What action could be taken to improve your performance in your current position by you?

A12. What action could be taken to improve your performance in your current position by your manager?

A13. What kind of work or job would you like to be doing in one, two or five years' time?

A14. What sort of training or experiences would benefit you in the next year?

A15. List the objectives you set out to achieve in the past period covered by this appraisal with the measures or standards agreed against each. Comment on achievement or otherwise with reasons where appropriate. Score the performance against each objective (1–3 = poor; 4–6 = satisfactory; 7–9 = good; 10 = excellent).

Objective	Measure / standard	Score	Comment
1.			
…10.			

A16. Score your own capability or knowledge in the following areas in terms of your current role requirements (1–3 = poor; 4–6 = satisfactory; 7–9 = good; 10 = excellent)

Time management		Meeting deadlines or commitments	
Communication skills		Team working or developing others	

Reporting and administration		Corporate responsibility	
Knowledge of products or services offered		Customer relationship management	
IT or equipment skills		Adaptability or flexibility	
Creativity and taking initiative		Dealing with pressure and work-load	
Problem solving		Decision-making	
Planning		Energy and enthusiasm	

A17. In light of your current capabilities, your performance against past objectives, and your future personal growth and/or job aspirations, what activities and tasks would you like to focus on during the next year?

Part B To be completed during the appraisal by the appraiser with appropriate discussion and validation.

B1. Describe the purpose of the appraisee's job. Discuss and compare with self-appraisal entry in A1. Clarify job purpose and priorities where necessary.

B2. Review the completed discussion points in A2-A14, and note the points of and action.

B3. List the objectives that the appraisee set out to achieve in A15. Score the performance against each objective (1-3 = poor, 4-6 = satisfactory, 7-9 = good, 10 = excellent). Compare with the self-appraisal in A15. Discuss and note points of significance, particularly training and development needs and wishes.

Objective	Measure / standard	Score	Comment
1.			
...10			

B4. Score the appraisee's capability or knowledge in the following areas in terms of their current role requirements (1-3 = poor, 4-6 = satisfactory, 7-9 = good, 10 = excellent). Compare scores with the self-appraisal in A16. Discuss and note agreed points training/development needs and wishes.

Time management		Meeting deadlines or commitments	
Communication skills		Team working / developing others	
Reporting and administration		Corporate responsibility	

Knowledge of products / services offered		Customer relationship management	
IT / equipment skills		Adaptability / flexibility	
Creativity and taking initiative		Dealing with pressure / work-load	
Problem solving		Decision making	
Planning		Energy and enthusiasm	

B5. Discuss and agree the appraisee's career options and wishes in A17 and note the agreed development aim(s):

B6. List the objectives that the appraisee should set out to achieve in the next period.

Objective	Measure / standard
1.	
...10	

B7. Discuss and agree the specific objectives that will enable the appraisee to meet required performance in current job.

B8. Discuss and agree the skills, capabilities and experience required for competence in current role, and if appropriate, for readiness to progress to the next role or roles. Note the agreed development areas, and the support for training and development to be given to help the appraisee meet the agreed objectives.

B9. Other issues:

Signed and dated by appraisee:

_____

and by appraiser:

_____

Table 15.3. Example record for a staff performance appraisal.

Potential investors will be keen to see this documentation, as it will help them better understand the workforce and see that care is being taken to monitor staff performance. A potential acquirer will have to take ownership of the team, so they want to see that HR has been diligent in managing the company's employees.

Equally, and in fact more importantly, regular appraisals can be really good ways to motivate and engage staff positively. They will feel like they are being valued and recognized for their efforts. They will have an opportunity to voice any concerns and also to be congratulated for their good work. It is also a chance to provide news about a bonus, a pay rise or a promotion, explaining why it has been given.

Retaining talent

Motivating staff in a company is also not just about money. Beyond the basic wage, it is possible to offer rewards and an environment that encourages staff to stay with the company and perform well. If they move on, they may lose many intangible benefits that they value highly and that may not actually cost you much as a company in cash terms.

Things to consider are many. For example, free tea and coffee in a kitchen costs almost nothing compared to the cost of running a business. Yet you will be giving staff time to mingle and talk, saving them money in a vending machine, and encouraging them to have more refreshments which may well improve their productivity. It may also be worth extending this benefit to include free juice or fruit, supporting a healthier lifestyle and making people happy at work.

You could also provide a library for staff to browse and borrow from, a regular newspaper, trade journals and a place to read them. Once again, these facilities can all benefit the business because staff will have an opportunity to catch up on relevant news, relax between work sessions, and, most importantly, talk to each other.

The offer of training is also valuable. If staff can spend time on a course that contributes to professional development, the change of scenery and chance to learn something new is often appreciated by the staff too. Examples can include first aid training, attending a trade show or participating in a conference. Keep a record of the staff training in their HR file which you can discuss at appraisal time and review new courses identified to keep each employee learning and developing. This record can also be used by staff for keeping track of their own continuous professional development (CPD) which may lead to qualifications like being an official member of a society or becoming chartered in their field. You may also decide it is company policy to promote this kind of membership and pay for one or more membership subscriptions to a relevant body on behalf of the staff.

You also need to be careful about benefits that are taxed. You will have to declare them and make sure your employees understand the impact. For company cars or private healthcare, you may well still feel they are valuable both to you as a business and to your employees.

Sometimes benefits can attract favourable tax savings, and it is well worth talking this through with an accountant or HR expert. For example, paying additional pension contributions in lieu of salary in the UK can save on some tax for both the employer and the employee, and some staff may really appreciate this refinement to their package.

It is also important for the company to undertake other activities that boost staff moral or make them feel part of a team (or even a family). Examples could include having a company charity that is regularly supported; both through fund raising activities, donations or through visits and staff interaction. Social activities like evening get-togethers, sports teams, a Christmas lunch, excursions and awaydays can be motivational, as well as educational or health-promoting, bringing instant benefit to the company and its productivity.

As a start-up, these initiatives may seem time-consuming and costly. However, start small and delegate their day-to-day organization to a member of staff that is excited by them, and they will start to take form without too much work from yourself. The aim is to provide the culture and environment in which staff are supported, cultivated and promoted.

Employee share options

Another good way to motivate staff is for them to be stakeholders in the business. In a company with shares, it can mean giving your employees shares or options to buy them. It is an area that needs careful thought, as there are tax implications for both the company and the individuals concerned, but a well-structured share-option scheme can enable employees to enjoy the success of the company encouraging them to work hard towards an exit. There are also other issues to consider, such as how big or small the share option pool is (ie, what the effective percentage of the company's equity is assigned to the employees; typically the range is from 5%–10% in a start-up so that there is still scope to attract investors and motivate the founders).

In Table 6.1 we considered a capitalization table at the stage of an early VC (venture capitalist) coming on board. This may also be a good time to create an employee share option plan (ESOP). Table 15.4 shows the table with an ESOP added in this round of funding, accounting for 6% of the company on completion.

The option price may be set at £20 per share (ie, the current value) so that an employee has the option to buy at this price later, ahead of an exit where the price is agreed to be higher, thus making a capital gain. This would reward the staff for progress going forward. Where an employee had been with the company for some time already, the strike price may be set lower (such as £1 or £5) and so the employee is already sitting on a paper gain for his or her hard work to date and remains motivated to further success.

The ESOP is set aside for multiple employees. It is up to the board and the trustees of the scheme to decide how many options (ie, shares) each employee is entitled to. So, for example, the ESOP illustrated has set aside 2000 shares. In a company of ten people, each may be assigned 100 shares (totaling 1000) with a particularly senior manager being assigned 100 shares more, so the pool has 1100 under option and 900 available. These available shares can be used for future recruits or used to top-up existing employees who perform well or get a promotion. Hence, the ESOP can be used as a way to boost cash salaries and bonuses without a direct impact on company cashflow.

However, value is only realized when the share options are exercised, so that the shares are bought and allocated, then the shares are sold, for example, during a trade sale or listing on the stock market. As an incentive, the scheme might be too long term and risky to suit everyone.

Investment round	Shareholder	Number of shares	Price per share	This investment	Investment to date	Post-money valuation	Ownership
0: incorporation	Founder 1	10,000	£1.00	£10,000	£10,000	£10,000	50%
	Founder 2	10,000	£1.00	£10,000	£10,000	£10,000	50%
	Total	20,000	£1.00	£20,000	£20,000	£20,000	100%
1: friends and family	Founder 1	10,000	£2.00	-	£10,000	£20,000	44.5%
	Founder 2	10,000	£2.00	-	£10,000	£20,000	44.5%
	Friend 1	2,500	£2.00	£5,000	£5,000	£5,000	11%
	Total	22,500	£2.00	£5,000	£25,000	£45,000	100%
2: angel investor	Founder 1	10,000	£5.00	-	£10,000	£50,000	38%
	Founder 2	10,000	£5.00	-	£10,000	£50,000	38%
	Friend 1	2,500	£5.00	-	£5,000	£12,500	9%
	Angel 1	4,000	£5.00	£20,000	£20,000	£20,000	15%
	Total	26,500	£5.00	£20,000	£45,000	£132,500	100%
3: early venture capital	Founder 1	10,000	£20.00	-	£10,000	£200,000	28%
	Founder 2	10,000	£20.00	-	£10,000	£200,000	28%
	Friend 1	2,500	£20.00	-	£5,000	£50,000	7%
	Angel 1	4,000	£20.00	-	£20,000	£80,000	11%
	VC 1	7,000	£20.00	£140,000	£140,000	£140,000	20%
	ESOP	2,000	£20.00	-	£0	£40,000	6%
	Total	35,500	£20.00	£140,000	£185,000	£710,000	100%

Table 15.4. The capitalization table up to and including the first round of venture capital investment with an ESOP.

Furthermore, the ESOP is not free money for the company either; you can see that the addition of the pool has diluted the share in the company of the other stakeholders. Existing shareholders have to agree that the scheme brings value to the company, and the investor coming on board will factor it into their investment too, as the pre-money and post-money valuations are of course adjusted. Note that in this case the VC drops from 21% to 20%, which may fit with their reporting requirements, so keep in mind that you can use the ESOP to your advantage during rounds of investment as well; it can help tune the valuation and show that you as a founder are encouraging your team to share in the company's success.

The exact way the ESOP is treated also needs professional advice; for example, are the shares issued to a trust? or authorized but not actually issued? and how are they shown on the company balance sheet? The voting rights and employee exercise rights also need to be carefully documented and followed appropriately.

Another issue is to handle properly what happens if an employee leaves at their own volition (for example, they find a new job), because of poor performance or because you have had to lay them off. These can be variously classed as 'good leavers' and 'bad leavers'. In the former, they may retain their options or shares for the work they have done, and in the latter case they may forfeit the benefit. Also, share options can work wonders when things are on the up, but employees quickly detect when things are not going so well and they may see all the accrued value for their hard work evaporate before their eyes as shares and options are only on paper; a medium that is easy to screw up.

Losing staff

When a member of staff does leave the company, the opposite of an induction should occur; a checklist needs to be run through to ensure property is returned (such as keys, computers, phones), contact information is up to date, final salary (including outstanding holiday pay) is processed, and surviving clauses of agreements are understood (such as confidentiality and non-compete). It is also important that relevant departments disable accounts (such as email, remote login, access to calendars, social media and so on). Email forwarding may need to be set so that the manager or replacement member of staff receives the leaver's business emails and phone calls. It will also be necessary to ensure share options, pensions, and subscriptions are processed properly.

Often it is beneficial to remain on good terms, as you never know when a past member of staff may reappear in your supply chain, across the table as a customer or in the room as a competitor. Equally, if they go away happy, they will still be a brand ambassador for you, perhaps recommending you to a future contact in the industry. They may also end up in a government or civil servant role in which they shape policy, so far better to have then as an ally than an enemy.

Invaluable capex

Buy some company branded coffee mugs and give them to each of your staff as they move on. That way, they will be reminded of you in their new place of work and it may just lead to a new customer. £5 per printed mug.

In short, recruiting, retaining and releasing staff is a time consuming and costly business for any company but in particular for a fast-growing start-up. Making sure processes are in place to handle the day-to-day management and motivation of staff is crucial, and can prevent costly mistakes being made. Although it is advisable to dismiss staff that are contributing poorly to the business, it is also necessary to handle those that leave through their own progression.

Take-away and to-do list

- Staff are often the principal factor that make a business succeed, as generally speaking a team is needed to execute on the strategy, ensure operations are smooth, troubleshoot issues and grow the business by interacting with customers. People management can make or break a small, growing business.

☐ Write and advertize job descriptions for new positions.

☐ Create a recruitment policy for interviewing and offering a job.

☐ Create an induction process for new staff.

☐ Put in place a structured performance appraisal process for staff.

☐ Consider an official and well-structured employee share option plan (ESOP).

☐ Create a process for when staff leave the company.

16.

BUREAUCRATIC NIGHTMARES

For the record

Maintaining orderly documentation about your company from the outset is a good policy, but getting bogged down in procedures and bureaucracy will grind you and your business to a halt. As an entrepreneur, you are unlikely to overdo paperwork because doing so often gets in the way of rapid progress. Bureaucracy is one of those things that is usually imposed and enforced by government bodies or middle managers of large organizations. Hence, when you start out, your new company is probably free of such distractions.

But it is worth having some structured procedures in place. By spending a little time on them at the start, they are easier to keep updated and to grow with the company. Then, before you know it, you (or your successor) will be able to become ISO 9001 quality accredited without much additional effort or pain. And when it comes to exit, all will be in order for a much smoother transition.

There are many ways to run a basic, functional and yet beneficial record-keeping system. Depending on your specific business, you can hone what you need to bring value to the business. In essence, the approach should be to logically systemize your business so as not to lose vital knowledge down the cracks. I outline some considerations here to get you started.

Documentation

Firstly, set up a simple system for the document names and numbers. I have experimented with this over time and within different companies, and have come to adopt the simple system already introduced: MyCo-CC-DN0000x.y (eg, MyCo-CC-DN00001.1, MyCo-CC-DN00136.3 and so on).

Therefore, in this system, the first controlled document you write would be called MyCo-CC-DN00001.1. You may remember this being your company information that we discussed earlier. The document will have a title, an author, an issue date, and, ideally, the name of someone else that has countersigned it. The latter will have read and understood the document and perhaps have suggested some further additions before it was finalized.

I have tried having different kinds of names instead of DN (meaning document number), for example DOC for general document, IND for induction, NDA for non-disclosure agreement etc. Although this method works, you can soon end up with a myriad of three letter acronyms and your staff will feel obliged to invent their own in time too. Also, you will have with some overlaps like POL for policy and PRC for procedure. You may not even know yourself the subtle difference, never mind your confused staff.

Therefore, I am of the view it is probably best just to have DN. I also think it is beneficial to include some leading zeros. So MyCo-CC-DN1.1 will be MyCo-CC-DN0001.1. I doubt you'll go over 1000 document types never mind 10,000, so the leading zero(s) help with keeping things neat and readable. You then need to maintain a simple list of the DNs issued. The number and title is usually enough at this stage, as any more information can be found on the document. Keeping this list up to date can be facilitated using a shared document on a server, perhaps with a link to the most up-to-date version of the document in question. If you want to be more ambitious, you could provide it on an intranet page or start using a simple document database. But these things can easily come later once you have the basic system in place.

The next thing to ensure is that the most up-to-date version is the one readily available and in use. Moreover, the documents should be read only (such as a pdf) and editable only by authorized people (you, the other directors, and, eventually, the appropriate managers and teams in certain departments). For example, an induction document should only be edited by certain people in the HR department.

This means it is worthwhile adding the department owner (in generic terms, not the person's name) to the database too for quick reference. This ensures that as your document list becomes longer, each department will be able to filter quickly which ones they are in charge of and ensure they are maintaining them appropriately.

Traceability

Keeping track of revisions is also important, especially in the future when there are many staff in the business and no one will know off the top of their head who had edited what. So, if you revise a particular document, for example, MyCo-CC-DN0001.1, then call the next version MyCo-CC-DN0001.2. The old version can then be moved to an archive so that it stays on file but is no longer used.

If you create a whole new document, you increase the DN number so as to call it MyCo-CC-DN0002.1, for example, and so on. In the end, you will have a list of current documents MyCo-CC-DN0001.1, MyCo-CC-DN0002.3, MyCo-CC-DN0003.1, MyCo-CC-DN0004.2 etc.

You can use this simple system to capture pretty much all your documents and templates. For example, these could be your policies, procedures, agreement templates, business plans etc. From the outset, you will have a matrix of who can edit them, as well as who can read them. This can also be added to your index sheet.

So that the system works in practice, keep a Word (or equivalent) document of each of the original versions, and a pdf copy of the current one. Any new drafts should also be available in the original directory, marked as 'draft' so that people know there is one in progress, but do not use it until it is ready. This is illustrated schematically in Table 16.1 and builds on the server structure that has already been introduced.

Top directory	Sub-directory	Typical contents
00-DOCS	00-ARCHIVE	Copies of old versions for reference. Keep original word versions rather than pdfs, Eg, MyCo-CC-DN0001.1 Title1.doc MyCo-CC-DN0001.2 Title1.doc MyCo-CC-DN0002.1 Title2.doc MyCo-CC-DN0003.1 Title3.doc, etc.
	01-DN	Index file: 00-KIQ-DN Document register. Documents: MyCo-CC-DN000x.y as Word and Pdf Latest versions only, eg, MyCo-CC-DN0001.3 Title1.doc MyCo-CC-DN0001.3 Title1.pdf MyCo-CC-DN0002.2 Title2.doc MyCo-CC-DN0002.2 Title2.pdf MyCo-CC-DN0003.2 Title3.doc MyCo-CC-DN0003.2 Title3.pdf Draft versions in progress for reference: eg, MyCo-CC-DN0001.4-DRAFT Title1. doc
	02-SA	Index file: 00-KIQ-SA Signed agreements register. Documents: MyCo-CC-SA000x as scanned signed pdf versions, limited access permissions, eg, MyCo-CC-SA0001 Title1.pdf MyCo-CC-SA0002 Title2.pdf MyCo-CC-SA0003 Title3.pdf

Table 16.1. More details about the practical workings of the controlled documents.

This system can work well for a small team. It only tends to be an effort to implement, as using the documents and making updates thereafter is hardly more onerous than not having a system at all. The fact that you have a pool of ready-made and generally correct documents that people can use is a great boost to efficiency.

As the business grows, the simple system of keeping the documents in a server directory can be enhanced by using a document control database, an online document manager or an enterprise resource planning (ERP) system. The great news is that you can drop your existing controlled documents into the new system and continue, so the important bit is having the system rather than worrying too much about the platform at the outset. And for the potential acquirer, they will see a process that they can take and integrate into their system without too much additional effort.

Other classes of records

The same thoughts apply for the other numbering systems that have been introduced; such as the asset number (AN) scheme, the signed agreement (SA) scheme and so on. It is also useful for the finance department to adopt a compatible scheme for their documents generated by the accounting software. For example, use IN for invoice, PO for purchase order (where used), DO for delivery order, CN for credit note etc.

One of the big problems with business is having a happy medium as far as bureaucracy is concerned. Start-ups are usually rather light on process, traceability and documentation. Scale-ups tend to introduce procedures in silos as new recruits realize from their own past experience that something is needed and hence a multitude of internal systems sprout up. Larger companies eventually have so many bureaucratic processes that they drive the good employees away. The latter situation tends to come about because there is a perceived need for tight controls in a complex organization that may have been burnt by fraud or a poor decision in the past. Also, directors in a small company tend to be able to keep an eye on everything, but much larger companies are necessarily more devolved to middle managers, divisions and departments.

Exit warrant

A trail of paperwork can help immensely with the necessary due diligence of an investor or acquirer. Firstly, the system makes it so much easier for the business owners to find all the documents for the investor to review, and, secondly, the investor sees that the business is well organized. Therefore, every time you lament the bureaucracy that you seem to have created within your own business, despite trying your best to avoid it, remember that it is there for the final exit when hopefully it will have been all worthwhile many times over.

Manufacturing and travellers

A time when traceability and document control plays a key role is in the case of production. The manufacturing of an item requires set processes to be followed and quality to be assured and tested. A good approach is to introduce a product traveller at an early stage. This is, at its simplest, a piece of paper (or virtual document) that moves along the assembly line as the product is being pieced together. This traveller outlines the process at each stage (perhaps calling on a particular DN for specific details) and can be used by operators to log information about test results (such as tolerances or calibration), initialing and dating either physically or electronically that they performed the necessary task. At the end of the line, the product is dispatched to the customer and traveller is filed so that the details of the production run can be reviewed if there is a future quality issue or warranty return. In such instances, TR is a good designation for a traveller such that the system is MyCo-CC-TRxxxx.y. This is illustrated in Figure 16.1.

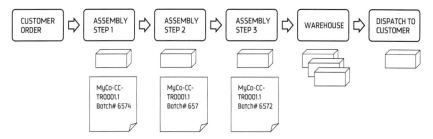

Figure 16.1. The traveller system helps define and control production. A copy of a specific process defined in MyCo-CC-TR0001.1 accompanies each batch of products and then is filed at the end of the line before dispatch. Note that the same MyCo-TR-TR0001.1 is called up for each batch, and an overall process improvement would result in MyCo-CC-TR0001.1 being archived and MyCo-CC-TR0001.2 being introduced after qualification and approval.

If a manufacturing start-up can monitor its production run in this way from early on, it will be able to scale much more quickly. This is because the manufacturing team will be able to deal with, and learn from, problems with product quality as issues arise. The company will in parallel build a very valuable record of its manufactured items. The same scheme can be applied to R&D as well, using travellers to define iterative experiments and log specific results. Indeed, an output from R&D should be the first version of travellers to be used for production.

Take-away and to-do list:

- Handling and controlling internal documents and processes need not actually be a bureaucratic nightmare, but it is a necessary evil. Try to keep things intuitive and useful so that staff use the system rather than avoid using it at all costs and invent their own.

☐ Ensure the DN system is tracking important documents and templates.

☐ Ensure the AN and SA system is also in place.

☐ Serialize financial documents in a similar way using.

☐ Create a system of travellers for any product manufacturing or assembly.

17.

DEFERRING TO THE BOARD

Board members

The company board is an interesting beast because few people fully understand its remit and responsibility. I think it is fair to say being a company director used to be seen as a badge of honour, and many would jump at it without realizing the legal ramifications.

A director is like a trustee of the company; someone that provides oversight and must act as the backstop. The directors need to know what is going on the company; they need to ask questions, constructively challenge colleagues and be confident that all is well.

So, as a founding director, much of this is fine as you are inextricably involved in everything that goes on. Hopefully, you understand who is doing what as the company grows. However, keeping on top of it all can be hard work. It is why some of the structures and ideas described in this book can be useful, if chaos is not to reign.

Having two members of the board can be useful in sharing the workload and providing two opinions for taking things forward. This could be a husband and wife or a board of two unrelated co-founders.

When investors join the company, they will often want to join the board. Interestingly, an investor we had in one company thoroughly understood the ramifications of being an official director, so actually came as an observer with rights to be elected as a director under certain conditions.

Equally, some minority investors may push to become board members. This may not be strategically wise for the company. For example, they may be a corporate investor (such as one of your company's strategic customers or suppliers, rather than simply a financial investor) in which case all the details discussed at board level may be too sensitive for them to hear. Also, as directors have voting rights, depending on the constitution, you could find yourself outvoted on something and having the frustration of not being able to steer the company in the direction you wish.

Therefore, to deter requests for a seat on the board, you could cite the legal ramifications. Note that observers generally have all the rights to read the board papers, minutes and attend the meetings, so they will have access to much of the information. However, they will not have the right to vote and nor will they have the legal responsibilities.

That said, it is beneficial to have a board of high-calibre and capable directors, especially for a rapidly growing start-up that may seek future investment or has the aim to exit with a high value. It gives a signal of good oversight and strategic planning, particularly if supported by board reports and minutes.

Board reports

In building value for an exit, its pays to use your board, provide written board papers in advance and document minutes of the meetings. Doing so is an opportunity to highlight successes, disclose issues and keep track of developments. The board report can follow a similar structure to the business plan and make reference to your organizational departments:

- Introduction: overall summary of the period being discussed, key developments and key milestones against those outlined in the business plan.

- Marketing update: developments in the market; progress with websites, social media and any analytics; and progress with literature, trade shows and press relations.

- The competition: any updates about competitor activities.

- Your product, service or technology: update on R&D, prototypes and product development, as well as intellectual property such as trademarks, design rights and patents.

- Customers: updates on business development, the sales pipeline and actual sales, as wells as any warranty issues or customer service aspects.

- Your team: overview of HR news including recruitment, changes in organizational structure, any key staff that have left or are underperforming. Again, relate back to your business plan in terms of milestones to see if you are on track.

- The finances: use the board report to present key financial information regularly. How much cash is left in the bank, what are the cashflow forecasts and how does the profit and loss and balance sheet look against projections. Use this section to highlight informative metrics such as staff costs, sales revenue, investment needs and so on.

- Next steps and the exit: finally, provide a conclusion on the current status of the company, the primary goals to aim for during the next reporting period and how everything aligns with the original strategy set out in the current business plan.

The board reports, agendas and minutes are therefore sensitive documents. They do not need a DN as they are one-off reports each time, rather than being live documents with version numbers. If you wanted, you could use DN as a means of setting the template. However, in reality you are likely to use the last board report, agenda or minutes as the template and edit it, so having another controlled document is unnecessary and this is where having too much bureaucracy can be avoided.

Board meetings

Board meetings should be set regularly, but monthly may be overkill if you are a small company with lots to do. We found that every two months worked well for our technology start-up in Singapore. This frequency provided enough time between meetings to get a lot done, and it was also regular enough to keep on top of developments. The issue with this timing, however, was that it did not always align with the traditional financial quarters, when investors expect their statements. So, either go for quarterly board meetings or have monthly meetings (or reports) but perhaps earmark every other one as a longer meeting for strategic matters to be discussed at more length.

Keeping records of attendees, apologies and the discussion in the form of minutes is excellent practice as well. These can be formally adopted by the board as a true record at the following meeting with matters arising dealt with accordingly. Having this full set of board material even in a small company can pay dividends. We made sure that we disclosed everything of significance in the board reports. When it came to due diligence for investment and the eventual sale of the company, we provided all the board reports and answered many of the warrants with the caveat that the investor or acquirer should read all the documented issues in the board report as part of the disclosure.

> **Exit warrant**
>
> Use your regular board report and minutes to document any issues within the business, as this is a good way to remember to disclose problems, seek advice and ensure that any warrants made to investors are complete as they can be provided with the documents to read.

Advisory board

A board of advisors is also a useful body to create. Having a list of say six to eight experienced experts displayed on your website brings gravitas to your company. Doing so shows customers, investors and competitors that you have the possibility of input from other business leaders. It further indicates that you may be seeking their advice over specific transactions, so it is not worth a prospective supplier or customer trying it on. For an investor or acquirer, the advisory board also shows that other experts have bought in to your plan and are happy to associate their name with yours.

The advisory board could consist of sector experts, technology experts, and investors that are not represented on the board of directors, as well as legal or intellectual property experts.

Invaluable capex

Send your board members and advisory board a branded coffee mug; you want them to have your company at the forefront of their mind, and others may enquire about your company to them during a refreshment break. No more outlay if you bought in bulk for a marketing campaign.

Of course, as a start-up, you will want to keep costs low, so it may not be possible to pay the advisors much, if anything. The key is to keep their workload low. Only ask them for advice when needed, but do approach them frequently enough to keep them engaged, updated and involved. They can be incentivized with small retainer fees, specific fees for agreed tasks, or commission should they bring in a sale. It may also be beneficial to involve them in the share option scheme as well. This will keep your cash costs manageable but also incentivize them to see opportunities that could lead to new customers.

You could also convene the board of advisors to meet as a group once or twice a year, perhaps before or after a board meeting so that they can interact with the directors as well. If the meeting is well structured, it can be used to provide an update of progress, to highlight areas where you need help, and to solicit advice and insight from the group. If the advisory board is high calibre, the members will also benefit from meeting each other.

In the case of Singular ID, our board of advisors included our business incubator landlord who was well connected in one of our target markets, our patent attorney, a technical expert from the US who had been the executive director of our research institute, an entrepreneur in the UK with whom I had worked in another technology start-up business, and a technical expert from the University of Oxford who had been my college tutor there when I was working on my doctorate. Hence, we had a diverse and highly experienced pool of advisors that were relevant to our business and located around the world in markets we were developing.

Ultimately, the board of directors and the board of advisors should be there to improve your decision making and seize opportunities whilst understanding any risks. Both boards can be reshaped as the company grows, but do make sure that members sign confidentiality agreements that survive their term, and that they are kept informed of progress so that they say and do the right things when acting as your ambassador out in the field.

Take-away and to-do list

- Having a board of directors with one or two independent non-executive members can lend credibility to the business and really help with strategic planning and execution. Augmented with a board of advisors, these bodies can add value to a business. If utilized constructively they can significantly aid the task of scaling up towards an exit.

☐ Convene regular board meetings.

☐ Write regular board reports emulating the structure of your business plan.

☐ Build a board of advisors to work synergistically with the board of directors.

18.

CYBER DANGER

The shadowy aggressor

About sixth months ago I had a phone call from the owner of a neighbouring business asking for a little advice. She had opened an email, clicked on a link, and now she was experiencing problems with accessing her files. Even her documents in the cloud, in this case Dropbox, were also unreachable.

She had inadvertently activated some malware in an unsolicited email called Cryptolocker, which had encrypted all her documents on her hard drive, as well as her cloud service. If she had not had a separate disconnected back-up, she would have lost everything, as even paying the bitcoin ransom was not guaranteed to get it all back.

Her business was relatively small. So, at least, she did not have a building full of staff connected to a common network that might also have become infected and lost everything.

It goes without saying that one of the greatest dangers to your business is a breach of your cyber security. It can cause immeasurable harm to your brand and distract you from the day-to-day demands of your business. It could also cost you a fortune in fines and lawsuits.

There are numerous threats to consider, and if you put in place some sensible policies right at the start, they will protect your business for the future and reassure your customers, your investors and ultimately your acquirers.

Company data

One of the issues to consider carefully is the information you collect about people and how it is stored and accessed. As a mimimum, you will be keeping personal information about your employees, directors and shareholders. You will soon have information about your suppliers, customers and about people in your network. Over time it will become more diverse, more encompassing and more valuable to others.

Equally, if you are an online business that sells to the public, you will be gathering large amounts of data relating to individuals including potentially their names, addresses, phone numbers and payment details. Depending on your product or service, you may also be processing usernames and passwords to provide online customer accounts with personal-profile information.

As a business, you will have the legal responsibility of keeping the data safe from being compromised by hacking, theft or loss through incompetence; and this remit extends to your staff and others with whom you may share information.

There are several things to get right from the outset: Make sure your staff are aware of the issue and treat data with utmost care. One obvious point is the use of mailing lists and just adding everyone as a CC on email. This practice exposes all the recipients to your mailing list which is not only valuable and confidential, but also annoys your recipients because they have had their email addresses widely shared. If they are private or personal emails, this could land you and your business in hot water.

If you process and store personal information, you will almost certainly need to be aware of local privacy laws. The EU is keen to safeguard privacy (for example the new GDPR or General Data Protection Regulation), and the UK has the Information Commissioners Office (ICO) with whom you may need to register your company.

Invaluable capex: a physical safe

Select a medium-sized safe that can be bolted from the inside to a wall so that it cannot easily be stolen wholesale. For example, fix it inside another large cupboard or cubbyhole so that it is generally out of sight. Select a digital keypad safe with a set of spare override keys. Keep one key in a safe place at home and another one in a safe place at work (or alternative site, such as a neighbour's house). Then set the safe to a memorable number, not the default 1234 or 8888. Outlay: £50.

Where and how you store information is also worth reviewing. Staff information is the domain of the Human Resources department, and should be filed carefully and securely. Hard copies such as signed contracts, interview notes, and so forth should be filed in a locked filing cabinet or cupboard. Electronic records should be in the respective department folder on the server, with the correct access permissions set and ideally the information should be encrypted.

Data servers

You also need to be aware that cloud services may store sensitive information in another country to where you are located, which can create problems. Firstly, it may actually be illegal for you to store personal or contract information away from your home country. Government contracts may insist that any data related to a project be stored in the home country: a cloud server may well distribute it to other jurisdictions either as a master copy or as back-up. Problems arise if your files are breached and information leaks out in the wrong country or into the wrong hands. It is also an issue because other governments may have the right to view and process data being stored within their shores. Your confidential information or the private information of individuals connected with your business could be used in the wrong way, making your company liable.

As such, you should consider where you are storing your data early on. Ideally, all your data should be encrypted, backed up and not reliant on a single server or supplier. For a small growing company, there are various security strategies that can be recommended.

You could host your own small server in a locked secure area in your business. Servers are not expensive (the price of a PC or laptop) and can provide extra flexibility and control. The issue is to ensure that it is maintained with software updates, that it is correctly configured from a security perspective, that it is encrypted in case it is breached or stolen, and that it has a back-up maintained on another site that is also set up in a similar secure fashion.

If you decided to use a remote cloud solution, ensure the service is backed up, that the content is encrypted, that the information is stored in a known territory and that you have local back-ups in case the service provider goes bankrupt or suffers a major breach of its own. Alternatively, you could back up to another cloud service run by a different organization.

If you are not an IT guru, setting this kind of the system up could be daunting, but ultimately if you can understand it and have followed some basic principles, you will be in a much better position to restore data or deal with new threats when they surface, for example, in the media.

When an investor or acquirer undertakes due diligence on your company, cyber security is likely to be one of their concerns. So much of the value they are buying is inextricably linked to data, so they will want to be sure it is safe and has not already been compromised. Because fines can also be high, they will be concerned that large chunks of their cash investment could be lost if data security is not sufficient.

Password protection

Passwords are a key aspect to security, as they will enable access to your files, services and, of course, unlock any encryption. Managing passwords can be difficult in a growing organization as soon there will be vast numbers of accounts requiring passwords, and a growing number of staff needing various levels of access to these files and services.

The good news is that if you put a basic system in place first, this will stand you in good stead and enable a future chief information officer (CIO) to take the reins when you can afford one.

Firstly, passwords need to be long and relatively complicated. They can still be memorable, but avoid short words from a dictionary because passwords tend to be guessed by hackers using dictionary-search algorithms. So, the longer they are, the more brute force will be needed to break them, as there are many more combinations to reach the correct one.

This can be further complicated by adding letters in upper and lower case, as well as numbers and symbols. The added complexity of making use of this wider character set is that this greatly increases the number of possible combinations.

A good approach is to substitute some numbers and symbols in place of letters in a long phrase where their similarity will help you remember them. For example, you could use a '5' or '$' instead of an 's'. Remember though that password-hacking algorithms are wise to this approach, so p4ssw0rd is not very strong; it is a known password that would be tried relatively quickly by a hacker.

Here is an example of a password:

- mnemonic: This book

- phrase: Start to exit by Adrian Burden

- first pass: StartToExitByAdrianBurden

- final pass: <$tart_TO_3xltBYAdrl4nBurden!>

- for a specific account:
  <$tart_TO_3xltBYAdrl4nBurden!>-MyEMAIL

- <$tart_TO_3xltBYAdrl4nBurden!>-MyWEBadmin

- <$tart_TO_3xltBYAdrl4nBurden!>-MyTWITTERfeed

I would not now use this example, but you get the idea. One key point is to use different passwords for different accounts, and do not follow an obvious pattern between them. Hackers are also well aware that if they crack an account with an email address and a password, that same combination will probably work in other services; for example, across Facebook, LinkedIn, Google Mail and Twitter. Software exists to automatically attempt these hacks and, in the case of a business, losing control of these social networking services one after another could be damaging.

Better still is to use truly random long strings of characters and perhaps store them on a password 'key chain'. The main point is to make sure the access to the master key chain is well protected, as if this is breached, all the accounts could in theory be compromised.

There is then the issue of ensuring all your staff also use strong passwords. Where you can insist on password strength, for example, in a policy on your own server, you need to ensure that the high levels of security are implemented. A server may then insist that any password is more than eight characters, consists of upper and lower case, and at least one number and symbol. It may also be possible to insist on two-factor authentication; where a password is entered, then a further code is delivered by email or text. This is common for internet banking, but becoming more widespread for logging into social media and cloud services.

Many services do not insist on rules, so a simple staff handbook entry about passwords and cyber security is recommended. Write down guidelines to which all staff must adhere and make it a disciplinary action if they are found not to comply. You may also want a policy that stipulates passwords are not shared and that they are changed regularly, such as every month or two. In reality, it can be difficult to enforce such things, so do not create rules that are overly arduous to follow. The principal aim is to protect key IT assets such as email, social media and servers, and assess the risk to them being compromised.

Strong passwords used by an educated workforce can make a business resilient against attack. Having a robust policy in place will comfort a potential acquirer of your business, as they will see that the risk to hacking is reduced even if they plan to introduce new policies of their own.

Social media security

The security of a business service on the internet is troublesome (for example, the company's Twitter or Facebook account). Firstly, you need to know who has access to it and the email that it is registered to. This step will ensure the account is retained if the member of staff managing it moves or changes job roll. The use of generic email addresses like 'socialnetworks@yourcompany.com' or 'marketing@ yourcompany.com' are useful. Having twitter@ or fakebook@ email accounts may not be so useful and usually the same people will be responsible for both. Multiple accounts mean more to manage and more to maintain and keep secure.

Making sure a list is maintained of all the accounts created for the company is difficult but highly recommended. Online services have created serious issues for business owners, as employees are quite capable of setting up a myriad of disparate accounts to try things out, such as a file-sharing service, a phone app or a project-management tool. This is fine, in principle, as trials of new software services could lead to more efficient ways of doing things within your organization. But you also need to ensure data does not leak from your business, or worse still get lost in the cloud when a member of staff moves on and no one knows how to access it.

Network and social media services all attribute value to your brand, so due diligence by an investor or acquirer will want to establish that your business has these services maintained, secure and under the full control of the organization. As a director, you may also need to warrant that passwords are retrievable by the business and there have not been any losses or breaches to date.

Personal devices

Another related cyber security issue is BYOD (bring your own device) when members of staff use their own mobile phone, tablet or laptop in your business. As a start-up, it can save a lot of money; why not just pay an employee for their business phone bills rather than the entire phone, and often people will buy quite expensive hardware for their own use anyway. The problem is that company data will end up on these devices, which could get damaged, lost or stolen. Not everyone will have implemented encryption, remote erasing or back-ups.

Company software or applications may have been bought for these devices and these could be lost from the business if the staff member leaves or their device is stolen.

Furthermore, these devices can be a backdoor into the organization. A phone or laptop without updated anti-virus software installed could pose a real threat to a company's network causing data to be erased, stolen or encrypted.

Once again, a clear policy is required and wherever possible consideration given to how the organization will grow and cope with an increasing number of diverse devices.

A good policy is to ensure that all devices are company owned and maintained and that personal devices are kept separate on, for example, a guest network at the company. Although this does create additional cost, it is a lot less than the potential cost of something going catastrophically wrong because a device is out of your control.

Remote data access

If you or your staff are working from home or on the road at hotels, cafes, train stations and airports, the use of a virtual private network (VPN) is encouraged. It will help to keep company information secure, as the device connects to your own organization through an encrypted channel so that people cannot eavesdrop on any communications or steal emails, passwords or documents. It will safeguard employees working from home, whose other family members may have infected computers on the network which could infect the business computer or intercept sensitive communications. Therefore, if you can setup a VPN service, employees can be instructed to make use of it both from home and whilst on the road.

As your company grows, so the number of staff away from their desk and in remote locations can increase dramatically. You want them to have easy access to business data so that they can effectively make sales and execute deals. So providing a secure means to reach data away from the business is vital, and investors will want to see that you have a scalable and robust system in place.

IT systems management

Managing a company's IT system, even a small one, can quickly become a full-time job in ensuring software is updated, anti-virus is in use, sufficient licenses exist for software that is installed, all the staff use the right software versions, and back-ups are maintained.

It is also necessary to ensure other hardware such as printers, routers, wifi access points, security cameras and internet phones have their default passwords changed and their security settings set appropriately. For example, management pages for the business router (gateway) device should not be visible on the external network, and any port forwarding to devices within the network should be well protected and monitored.

A major weakness in cyber security is the human factor; employees need to be trained to understand the threats and risks, and they also need to be managed so that they do not take shortcuts. For example, copying commercial data on to a portable hard drive to take home then losing it on the way. Or using a memory stick on a conference computer to show a presentation then it becoming infected with a virus. Also, disgruntled employees can cause harm unless their exit is well managed.

To help you improve cyber security, there are schemes such as Cyber Essentials in the UK that outline some technical controls to implement so that your system is more secure. There are also information assurance standards such as ISO 27001 or IASME Governance that can be obtained when procedures and controls are put in place. However, as a quickly growing start-up or scale-up, these certifications can feel daunting because your operating structures are changing rapidly as new corporate functions begin, production ramps up or overseas offices are opened.

Exit warrant

Good cyber security will enable you to warrant that breaches have not been made and that company information is safe. Robust policies will also help to ensure that the business is less likely to fall foul of laws governing privacy and data protection laws that are becoming ever more onerous for business owners and directors.

Disaster recovery

An important aspect of both cyber and physical security is to have a plan for disaster recovery in place. It can start off as a simple document that outlines potential risks such as power cuts, fire, theft and data breach, providing an assessment of what the implications will be and how to recover quickly. Going through this process can identify ways to mitigate disaster.

For example, a short power cut may not be a major problem for individual workers because their laptops will continue to function on their battery. However, the server, internet router and internet phones may need to have some uninterruptable power supply added to ensure systems still work for a while and data is not lost by a sudden power outage.

Think through other consequences. A fire will be easier to manage if you have offsite back-up of your data and a theft can be prevented through the use of encryption. Make your back-ups regular and isolated, as you do not want the virus to encrypt the computer and the only back-up at the same time. Also consider how you would rescue a locked account like Twitter; has an alternative company email address been provided or a company phone number? What about if there is a breach and confidential data is stolen that maybe relates to a third party (ie, your supplier's confidential information): do you have insurance for this kind of eventuality?

Another issue with cyber security is that you may fall victim because of your relationship with another party that suffers a breach. This could be your bank account; money could be moved from your account or the bank's services may be interrupted so that you cannot make or receive a payment. Similarly, your supplier may suffer a cyber security attack and lose some of your confidential information or simply be unable to fulfil an order.

Cyber security issues will unfortunately having increasing impact on your business. If you can build in redundancy and resilience even at the start-up stage, it will be good for your company's future. Investors will be keen to see a well-thought through disaster recovery plan, because they want their money to be spent on growing the business, not being wasted dealing with an unforeseen crisis.

Take-away and to-do list

- Managing cyber security in a growing business with a host of different staff from a variety of backgrounds each with their own device is a challenge, particularly as it is a field subject to high levels of complexity and change.

☐ Create a password policy for all staff that ensures every account has a different and complex password.

☐ Create a cyber security risk register and a disaster recovery plan.

☐ Encrypt data.

☐ Back up data to offsite and unconnected repositories.

☐ Take legal advice if you operate in different territories or your customers are located there.

☐ Use anti-virus on computers, servers and smartphones.

☐ Create a register of devices so that they can be maintained and updated.

19.

INTELLECTUAL PROPETY RIGHTS
(& WRONGS)

Imitation and flattery

A few years ago, I wrote the following phrase as an online introductory paragraph to the Malvern Festival of Innovation: 'today we need to innovate more than ever: the way we do business, the way we use resources; the way we live. We need new ideas to stay competitive, new technologies to improve lives, and new insights to lead the way. Join us to discover what's coming next, to learn how others are innovating, and to showcase your own research and development'.

A couple of years later, I became aware that another innovation festival had published the following on their website: 'innovation is changing the way we live. We need new ideas to stay competitive, new technologies to improve lives, and new insights to lead the way. The --- Festival of Innovation wants to showcase what's coming next, and how --- is already leading the way'.

I was astounded. The irony of it promoting an event about innovation was not lost on me. I used waybackmachine.com to see if there was a record of my website text from early on, and indeed I could establish that in September 2012 my text was in place. I used the same technique to confirm that their website was published later. Then I sent them an email and asked them to change the text which they duly did.

I also tried googling my entire phrase: 'we need new ideas to stay competitive, new technologies to improve lives, and new insights to lead the way'. I discovered it was now being used in marketing material and even ascribed as a quote from another person associated with the event. Since then, the phrase has also been used by another organization promoting another innovation event in another part of the world altogether. Imitation may be the sincerest form of flattery, but it detracts from your own hard work, can lead to customers being lost and maybe unlawful.

Intangible value

Aside from phrases, paragraphs, leaflets and white papers, all businesses generate wide-ranging and valuable intellectual property (IP). Indeed, the tailored systems and procedures that you are creating and implementing will form part of your own company's IP in the future.

Furthermore, your customer contacts, your business model and your market knowledge are also your IP. However, this low-level IP is really know-how that cannot easily be protected other than either keeping it a secret or making sure that it stays within the four walls of your company.

A problem with trade secrets is that staff come and go from an organization and they can take valuable information with them. This can of course be both intentionally and simply by default for having been immersed in your business for a while.

A first line of defence is to ensure that employees and contractors have signed agreements to keep your company information confidential and to instruct them not to use it for purposes other than progressing your business. Certainly, you want to make it clear that employees are not at liberty to set up on their own, go to a competitor or make use of your IP.

Investors and acquirers will also want to see that you have put non-compete agreements in place with staff. Although these only really stand up in law if they are a short-lived and reasonable. A non-compete clause of three to six months might be reasonable assuming they really were exposed to valuable knowledge and paid a salary commensurate with their responsibilities. To be effective, you need to put these provisions in place early on in your company's life and be clear through staff training what you consider is valuable IP that needs to be protected.

Keeping trade secrets is difficult and risky. If something is disclosed even in error, the business could suffer immeasurably and suing an individual after the event for negligence will likely not yield enough compensation to make up for it.

IP protection

As you are probably aware, there are other ways to protect IP in law around the world. These include copyright, trademarks, design rights and patents. There are plenty of books and resources available about what each of these are and how they can be used to protect ideas, but as an entrepreneur who will perhaps rely on IP to create value within the business, there are a few useful aspects to understand.

Firstly, protecting high-level IP using legal frameworks can be expensive. Patents can become costly because not only do they need to be carefully drafted by an expert to withstand scrutiny and attack in the future, they will also need translating, maintaining and filing in numerous territories to confer a reasonable level of worldwide protection.

Therefore, your business will need to have a long-term financial budget in place for IP protection, particularly if you are to develop a global brand, a distinctive product or an innovative device.

Secondly, by the nature of IP frameworks, you are publishing your know-how for your competitors to review and potentially improve or circumvent. In the case of patents, it means divulging recipes, parameters and methods that describe how your products work. With this in mind, when we drafted patents in our start-up, we also made sure that we included a range of options that would work so that the optimum was not necessarily obvious. Our writing technique was also to include a fair amount of descriptive prose that made the patent harder and longer to read, thus making it difficult for potential competitors to see the wood for the trees.

Thirdly, it is important to understand that truly worldwide protection is not achievable for a small enterprise. Much of the paperwork that costs dearly is not itself enough to defend your rights. As such, you need to develop an IP strategy that you can tune as you grow, being aware that deadlines and mis-steps can lock you out of options in the future. It is therefore well worth seeking some professional advice early on and having access to a patent lawyer who gets to know your business and understands your products or services.

Good practice

There are a few basic steps that can be put in place early on that will not cost you money and will help protect your IP. Firstly, whenever an employee writes some text, be it website content, a marketing brochure, software code, a business report and so forth, be sure to add a copyright symbol with the year of origination and the legal owner (usually the company name, eg, '© 2020 My Company Ltd).

Keep a record of the original article, even if it is an electronic copy on your server, so that should someone start duplicating your text, you can ask them to stop and you have a record of when you first created it yourself. This is where the DN document control system can come in useful. Be sure as well that you only copyright your company's original work.

It is also beneficial to have a process in place to monitor your IP and to act if it is being misused or abused. As a small company, this can be difficult, because you are unlikely to have a legal enforcement department. However, it can become a simple job for the marketing department to monitor with a service like Google Alerts. They can flag up mentions that may be an infringement of your own rights. The objective is to build this into the function of the department so that they routinely keep an eye out for problems and then you can act quickly and appropriately.

Trademarks need not be registered, but doing so affords much stronger protection. Again, seeking advice is important for your own situation, but beware that you generally have to be active in a market to enforce a trademark, so trademarking your device in the US when you do not sell your product there may not be much help. Equally, you have to link your trademark to one or more classes, so you cannot generally trademark something for every use and expect to be protected; it is why you sometimes see the same trademark for quite different products in the same market. It is probably wise to apply for a registered trademark for a company logo or product name in the markets in which you are operating; as a start-up this is likely to be your home market, extending to a few other territories as you scale.

If you are using your own unregistered trademark, use the letters TM to indicate this. When a trademark is registered, you will need to make sure that marketing use the logo with the ® symbol on all your collateral. You will, therefore, need to be able to find all of its occurrences in existing documents, on stationery and online to add the new symbol. Going forward, the logo files, letterheads and so on will all need to be modified with the registration mark.

You will also need to be sure that this symbol is only used in jurisdictions where it is registered and that where possible you state that the logo, phrase or word as indicated is a registered trademark of your company.

Some similar considerations are needed for patents as well Once an application is made, you should add the words 'patent pending' where possible somewhere on the device, as well its paperwork and instruction manual. Then, when the patent is granted, you should normally state the applicable patent numbers on the item and in any documentation. Once again, this action needs coordination between R&D, production and sales, so keeping records will help make the change quickly and accurately.

Managing IP

As you write patents, file applications and register your IP, be sure to keep records of all the correspondence and associated paperwork. As with earlier discussions, you will end up with both electronic and hardcopy documents, so you will need a system for both formats.

> **Invaluable capex**
>
> Buy some picture frames for your certificates relating to company incorporation, trademarks, patents etc, as these can be displayed in your reception to remind staff and visitors alike about the value you place on creating and protecting IP. £10 per frame.

Managing a portfolio of IP also needs attention to detail. Hopefully, your appointed patent lawyer will take on much of the responsibility, because soon you will have a myriad of deadlines associated with responses to the patent office, renewals and further applications around the world. Each patent, for example, will grow into a family of different versions in different territories, each requiring defence, maintenance and renewal. Miss a deadline in a jurisdiction and the patent could lapse, which could be costly. Having an organized file with a calendar of key dates and a spreadsheet of key costs will help.

In-licences and sub-licences

Some technology companies may in-license other technology as well as sub-license their own out to others. It is often the case when a spin-off company from a university in-licenses the patents that were filed during an earlier research project.

This activity requires some time-consuming management as licence agreements need to be carefully crafted, but, equally, the results can be lucrative as they may drive sales or bring significant licensing income. A key consideration is to look to the future; ensure any in-licensing deals can be renewed and extended so you are not cut out later when you have made significant investment, but are not burdened with costs in the early years. Also consider whether you will need to sub-license what you are in-licensing. This is very likely to be the case for a technology company building on some university IP.

Similarly, when sub-licensing, you will need to be careful that you do not sign away worldwide exclusivity in perpetuity; rather limit the territories, time horizons and the scope of exclusivity so that the licensee can come back later if they are doing well, but you can involve others to tackle other market opportunities if they are not performing as you hoped.

Investors and acquirers will pore over the fine print of license agreements because they are often the backbone of your business value, especially early on. One thing an acquirer will want to be sure of is that licences apply to successors and assigns, because they could well fall into this category if they acquire the organization.

In the case of technology businesses, especially biomedical companies where protection is vital whilst lengthy trials take place, licence agreements will need to have long-term provisions so that profits can be extracted. Venture capitalists will be thinking about this in terms of their upfront investment, and acquirers will be considering it all based on the purchase price of the company.

Exit warrant

Keep a record of all your IP developments, including how things like patents are progressing through the system. It should include both positive and negative feedback so that the investor or acquirer is aware of any issues upfront. Make a point of including a section about the status of your IP in the regular board reports, as this way any issues will be clearly declared for current and future investors.

Counterfeiting

Another aspect to consider is the problem of counterfeit (fake) products. The whole business of Singular ID was built on addressing this issue. Ironically, we too suffered from third parties attempting to counterfeit our products. In fact, we even had a company approach us from southern Italy that had copied our logo and marketing material with a view to us partnering with them to do business in and around the Mediterranean region.

As a start-up, you may think that the problem of counterfeits is far away in the future, but if you manufacture a successful product, it is surprising how quickly knock-offs appear. Counterfeiters know that you are unlikely to spot them doing it quickly, so they will be able to get a head start in perhaps distant markets (like China or India) that you may not target for quite some time.

Therefore, try to anticipate these problems from the outset. Strategies include adding serial numbers to your products so that they are each identifiable, attaching overt and covert anti-counterfeiting features to make them harder to copy, and using customer service to engage with purchasers of genuine products (such as warranty registration or customer loyalty schemes). These brand-protection approaches actually become brand-enhancing activities, so can really build value in a company. Adding anti-counterfeiting features to products at launch means that there will be no legacy products in circulation that do not have the same features. This in turn avoids customer confusion and it is easier to educate the client what to look out for in your genuine product if you have been doing it all along.

Is IP everything?

Investors in tech companies like to see patents. They tend to overlook their cost in favour of the tick in their due diligence box for adding protection to their investment. Acquirers also like IP protection because they are buying something other than a secret that may already have got out.

Strategically, it may therefore be wise to put in place a few patents or patents pending before seeking investment or negotiating a trade sale. Potential investors and acquirers will look at the patent portfolio and associated IP with a view to understanding its value, which is often intangible, because much of it will be realized in the future.

Therefore, you being able to show a strong portfolio of protection and/or some licensing revenue where applicable can be a real boost.

And knowing the patent lifetime and the territorial scope can enable you to infer levels of future revenue which can increase the value of your company so that investors pay more for a given share or acquirers pay more for the entire business. As an entrepreneur, it could make a significant difference to you, as IP draws the eye away from the standard metrics of present price-earnings ratios to more fantastical numbers in the future.

Take-away and to-do list

- IP does not need to be an expensive asset to maintain, but it is far better if you identify what might be of value in your business and put a strategy in place to protect it. Ensure that any measures taken are budgeted going forward and maintained in current and future markets. Be ready to take action as soon as infringement is detected, even if it is a simple cease-and-desist letter.

☐ Create a simple IP strategy that details what you will copyright, trademark, patent or protect.

☐ Task marketing with the job of monitoring for potential infringement of your IP, for example, by others misusing your company name, product name or marketing collateral.

☐ Create an anti-counterfeiting or brand-protection strategy for new products or services.

20.

SALES CLOSE TO THE WIND

Generating revenue

I vividly remember drafting the first sales contract for our anti-counterfeiting technology product. We were in the very early stages of the start-up and securing an initial customer was a critical milestone for us to lend credence to both our new technology and our proposed business. My co-founder and I agonized over the structure of the payments, but finally we decided to ask for an upfront payment, a couple of staged payments and then a final payment. This proposal was accepted and the series of payments helped ease the cashflow immensely, as we were otherwise funded with venture capital with lots of overheads and no revenue stream other than an R&D grant.

This initial sales lead had come from coverage in the national media of our recent press release announcing that we had spun off from the research institute to commercialize a new technology. It just goes to show that 'sales and marketing' should really be marketing then sales.

Making time for both activities in a business is vital, but make sure that you and your team understand the difference. A sales process which actually closes deals and brings in revenue is the lifeblood of your business, whereas marketing is an often open-ended activity that makes everyone feel busy but is not in itself going to generate any income.

If you are a shopkeeper or e-commerce site, your sales process is relatively simple; that of sourcing product to resell. That does not mean it is not without risk, as things can most certainly go wrong.

Your supplier could be unreliable or their product could give rise to warranty return issues. Or you could take on too much stock and find it difficult to shift inventory because it has become outdated or too expensive as the market moves on. As such, you need to forecast demand, price competitively but at a level that is profitable, and know your target market to ensure there is strong demand for what you wish to sell.

Things can get a little more complicated where you are selling a service because this generally involves costing your or your staff's time. This metric can be difficult to estimate because of unforeseen issues or delays. If your project involves consultancy and systems integration, you have the added technical unknowns and may experience problems with the system components being commissioned. An example would be the provision of a new IT system to someone; you may need to integrate the new computers into their network and unless you research it properly at the estimation and project-scoping phase, you could discover difficulties in a legacy system that add unforeseen costs to your project.

Quoting for sales

Your aim in scaling your business is to build a sales process that ensures that you and your team scope potential projects carefully. A system needs to be in place to cross-check time and cost forecasts, add suitable margins for overheads, contingency and profitability, and yet still produce a competitive and appealing quotation.

Winning a project based on time, cost and quality is as much an art as a science, and it is why good sales people can be hard to find. However, there should most definitely be rigour to the process so that costly mistakes are avoided.

Invaluable capex

Equipping a salesperson with an iPad or other tablet could be a better choice than a laptop, as they tend to be easier for a client to view and they can be shown a product presentation, catalogue or website at their own pace. £300–£500 outlay.

In the start-up phase, there are real pressures to secure your first customer contracts, and there is much uncertainty because you or your team may not have delivered a similar (or any) project previously. Equally, you must be careful not promise too much, as it may result in a failed project, lots of cost without payment or simply an unhappy customer. A satisfied customer is always gratifying, but having one in the start-up phase is beneficial beyond just the revenue generated because they can be used as a reference case. This may lead to a positive testimonial from which further customers can be secured.

I think that a good approach for a sales process is to create a customer folder for the present and future sales team to consult, keeping dated documents and correspondence filed there as a record. When a quotation is created, give it a number and version in the same manner as we have described previously, MyCo-QN-0001.1 and so on, where QN is the acronym used for a Quotation.

Base your quotation on as much rigour as possible. It is always useful to have a cost model derived from your business plan. The cost model should capture the prices for the various components of the quotation. So, if you are just selling a product, it is easy; something like cost times multiplier to cover overheads and profit. Note of course that deriving the multiplier is more complicated than it sounds. You need to consult your business plan for associated costs (apportioned for your utilities, salaries, buildings, business rates, taxes like VAT etc).

With a consultancy project, the model will include hourly rates, travel and subsistence, and other out-of-pocket expenses, such as the cost of trade reports you may need to source.

As projects become more complex, such as system integration or the delivery of a new product, so you will have to tabulate component costs, the bill of materials, assembly and testing costs, and so on.

Clearly, in the early stages, you may well be prepared to win a loss leader. This means that you will deliver a project at a loss so that you gain something intangible as well. For example, there might be a good chance of a larger future order, or a reference case that will enable your business to penetrate a new market more quickly. However, a loss leader still requires plenty of care in producing the quotation: ideally, it should not cost you cash (make your losses in terms of time or your value add, not buying something and simply selling it on at a lower price).

During the negotiating of sales projects, you have the opportunity to seek agreement to add extra beneficial terms, as doing so later may be much more difficult. For example, if you would like to use a sales project as a future case study set out this intention early on. A term could be included to outline that the customer agrees to provide a joint press release on signing, a testimonial on delivery, or to allow their name to be used in a case study at some point in the future. To allay their fears, you could say a case study or press release will be drafted for both parties to review and mutually agree, and that 'agreement to publish will not be unreasonably withheld'. Better still, draft the press release as an embargoed appendix in the initial sales document so that it is signed off as part of the sales process.

Discounting and payment terms

A key point with new quotations is that you are setting the tone for the future. So, where prices are discounted, it is worth showing this so that the customer understands that future prices may not be quite so appealing. It can be useful to use phrases like 'introductory discount', 'beta-version discount', or 'volume discount'.

Price is not everything, because delivery time and product or service quality also appeal to the client. Use these other factors to keep your prices higher from the outset, as it is much easier to reduce prices in the future than increase them. Therefore any quotation could usefully include information about how your product will be tested, guaranteed and delivered on time. Of course, these promises need to be kept, and any warranty needs to be carefully considered so that it is not too onerous for your business in the future.

I also think that a good way to offer a discount is through early payment. In a start-up or scale-up phase, it will greatly help your cash flow, so rather than quoting a payment term of 30 or 60 days, offer a small discount (say 5%) if the payment is made within say 7 days. Note that VAT needs to be carefully managed in these situations; legislation changed recently on how VAT is calculated in the UK for early payment discounts, so if in doubt, talk with your accountant before sending the quotation.

As we found with complex projects, it is helpful to stage the payments. Firstly, try to work in an upfront payment. Ideally, it will go some way to covering your initial outgoings, such as component costs, and so greatly improve your own cashflow and reduce your financial risk. Then indicate some staged payments as delivery occurs; for example, a payment after first installation or a delivery of a component. This will help you structure the delivery plan so that it creates incremental benefit for the customer and thus justifies you being paid for the milestone.

A final payment can then be structured after customer acceptance against a set of criteria; once the customer ticks a series of boxes to say everything is working as specified, the balance is paid.

In a large project, a good approach would be a 20% upfront payment, a series of staged payments making up the bulk of the project value (say about 70%) and the final payment of 10% on customer acceptance. In such circumstances, you also need to ensure that any agreements for the project state that the goods remain your company's property until paid for in full as agreed and that title does not transfer to the customer until then.

A caveat to this approach is that such upfront payments need to be carefully accounted for, both in terms of accruing for a project not yet completed and also because that money will almost certainly need to be refunded if delivery is not completed.

Overstretching the business

In Singular ID, we were once close to running out of money just before we accepted the first major sales project. My co-founder and I had an emergency discussion with our angel investor about the issues of taking on the work. We were worried about all the liabilities the contract would bring with it until delivery, and our associated concerns about not being able to pay future debts when they were to fall due (ie, becoming insolvent). In the end, we agreed that we were not yet insolvent, and that the prospects of securing future funding were good, but they were even better if we won this first customer project. It turned out to be the right decision and the process made sure we read and re-read what we are promising to deliver so that there was as much confidence as possible in what we were proposing.

Exit warrant

Investors and acquirers will want to know that there are no unlimited liabilities out there that may come back and bite. Therefore you will be asked to confirm that all sales have been made with limited warranties and with adequate insurance. If you have changed insurer during the lifetime of the company, previously sold products may not be covered. The best way to satisfy due diligence of this nature is to have all the sales agreements to hand with notes about any significant undertaking.

A key lesson here is that your terms need to be carefully drafted to ensure that you do not end up in hot water. Firstly, ensure that you only promise what you can deliver in terms of specification, time frame and price.

Then, make sure that your payment terms are clear and set against an unambiguous set of criteria in each case. Finally, ensure that any warranties and limitations of liability are clearly set out, and that any licence agreements (for example, if you are supplying software, some kind of recurring service or an IP-related product) are provided.

Delivery and transfer of ownership is also important, so ensure that delivery costs are detailed (for example, set out whether you include shipping and installation, or if delivery is ex-works which means to your factory door, or to a depot or port only). With large projects, you may need to consider insurance during transportation and delivery, prior to installation and acceptance. You may also have issues round export licences and import duties.

Sales of products and services also brings with it future liabilities; things can go wrong as products can malfunction or the advice given can be bad. So a cost of doing business is having sufficient liability insurance in place for your products and services. Your insurer will need to know details of the product or service in terms of how it works, how it might fail and what the customer is using it for and where. They will also need to know the territorial scope of their insurance, as providing cover to overseas customers can significantly complicate matters, especially in a litigious country like the US.

Clearly, an individual sales project in a particular company is going to have specific issues and concerns, but as a business owner, you need to put in place the system that makes this process as risk free and streamlined as possible. After all, it is the sales process that underpins the entire enterprise.

Sales knowledge

As sales become more routine for your business, acceptable policies in terms of what works for both you and your customer will become clearer. Hence recording these considerations as a decision tree in a spreadsheet, for example, can be helpful for the sales department to learn from each transaction. This dynamic document can be continuously updated so that the organization has a growing internal knowledge of what has been considered, tried and tested.

Often a customer will negotiate specific terms of a complex contract, so any variations agreed need to be carefully considered in terms of their financial impact. Equally, these special conditions should probably not find their way into the standard set of terms and conditions, but be there in the background as a fallback position for future negotiations with others. The process can be facilitated by making use of the document number (DN) system for the current set of standard terms and conditions, and then maintaining a sales log for a specific customer of any variations to the terms with some accompanying notes of the background justification.

Scaling sales quickly

Ultimately, you want your company's sales process to be well oiled, clear and with as little risk as possible. It will enable you and your team to sleep well at night, and for your business to generate new sales quickly and build on those that have gone before. High-tech product companies will face the greatest hurdles to this goal because of the ongoing complexity, but with a little care early on, it should be possible to achieve.

It is also always better to walk away from sales projects that are simply too risky or too complicated, or outside the usual scope of business.

Investors will want to see that a business can generate sales and that there is plenty of room to grow. Information about the potential market is one thing, but in reality, they will want to see that hard cash is being generated. During due diligence, they will almost certainly want to speak with customers and understand from them what value they see in your offering, and also what the experience of dealing with your business was like. Having some friendly, happy customers that will be amenable to talking with your potential investors will certainly smooth the way forward.

Take-away and to-do list

- Sales are a vital part of the business and in the start-up phase, they may be sporadic and risky. However, putting in place a system that allows new sales to be made using as much of the collateral and learning from previous ones is an efficient way to scale a business. Make sure you only promise what you can deliver and focus on time, cost and quality.

☐ Create a sales pipeline that funnels prospects through different stages, using something like Microsoft Excel in the first instance but migrating to another software platform or ERP system later.

☐ Start a document control system in the format MyCo-CC-QTxxxx.y to track quotations provided by your business.

☐ Ensure standard terms and conditions, warranty documents, end-user licence agreements and other sales-related documents are controlled using the MyCo-CC-DNxxxx.y system.

21.

BUTTONS, KNOBS AND THE DASHBOARD

In the cockpit

If you have been following the story so far, then you may well be feeling a little overwhelmed by the number of things you need to watch as a business starts and grows.

In many ways, it would be good if you could sit on a flight deck and have all the switches, dials and levers to pilot your business from take-off to exit with plenty of information to hand about how things are faring. It would also be good if you could level off at some point and let autopilot take the strain, but I am afraid that in the start-up and scale-up world, you are more likely to encounter a dogfight than an opportunity to cruise at altitude.

The good news is that some level of business instrumentation can be achieved by setting up your own private web page with ready-made links on it to the various social media, websites and online assets you use to run your business. It does not require a financial outlay, as you can make use of a free Google site, for example, and set it up as a private website (ideally shared with key members of your team). You can always migrate it to your own intranet later if you want to keep it all in-house and secure.

Business instrumentation

A typical dashboard set-up would include a direct link to your website's homepage, the website administration control panel, webmail and the web hosting platform. Then you should provide links to your social media channels. Other links could be to your bank and frequently used services for example at the tax authority (Government Gateway in the UK).

There could also be links to key infrastructure and building management systems, such as the device management pages of the router, the printer, the wireless access points, webcams and so on. All of these services are password protected, so even if you share the dashboard with other employees, they will not be able to access the specific services unless they have the security details to do so.

Exit warrant

Investors and potential acquirers like to understand the various company assets that are in use, so being able to show an intranet or dashboard which acts as a central portal to allow staff to access services easily can be a dealmaker.

A good way to start the construction is to pull it together based on the departments within the company, and create links to other web-based services or devices on your intranet. Over time you can embed 'widgets'. These tools could include news feeds and even more complicated scripts of code that show certain company figures (like sales in real time or the balance of your bank account, limited to certain users as appropriate). Figure 21.1 gives an example.

```
┌──────────────────────────────────────────────────────────────────────┐
│                                                                        │
│  Dashboard                                                             │
│                                                                        │
│                                                                        │
│  My Company Ltd                                                        │
│  Company short code: MyCo                                              │
│                                                                        │
│                                                                        │
│  Corporate              Website                    Planning Resources  │
│  Government Gateway portal   ISP hosting           Business plan       │
│  Companies House portal CPanel domain management   Company roadmap     │
│  Pension provider       Wordpress admin            Basecamp            │
│  Bank login             Website                                        │
│                         Webmail                                        │
│                                                                        │
│  Marketing              Analytics                  Office Network      │
│  Mailchimp              Google Analytics           Gateway Router      │
│  Eventbrite             Google Webmaster           Managed Switch      │
│  Wordpress Blog                                    Wi-Fi Access Point  │
│                                                    CAM1 (Entrance)     │
│                                                    CAM2 (Reception),   │
│  Social Networks        Affiliate Marketing        CAM3 (Car-park)     │
│  Twitter                Amazon Associates          Laser Printer       │
│  LinkedIn               Google AdWords                                 │
│  Facebook                                          Services           │
│  YouTube                                           VOIP phone          │
│                                                    Electricity supplier│
│  SUBPAGES: PROCESSES  WEBPAGE NOTES                                    │
│                                                                        │
└──────────────────────────────────────────────────────────────────────┘
```

Figure 21.1. Example screenshot of a simple company dashboard
of hyperlinks to various services and devices.

Company intranet

The advantage of the dashboard as a central portal to reach a range of separate services is that if someone leaves or is unreachable, the nature of the service is still obvious and it is not forgotten about. It is, therefore, a good way to control multiple aspects of your business from one place. You can also add other pages for specific departments or for specific tasks to help with workflows or departmental responsibilities.

As with all these systems, they can evolve as the company grows. Eventually, you may end up with an ERP system or series of intranet pages that include lots of company metrics that can really help your business extract information from your own server. However, the beauty of many cloud services is that a simple link can open a page of quite detailed information, like the Google Analytics of your website, for example.

Invaluable capex

A dynamic screen as an information board in a reception or office showing analytics (or twitter feeds and industry news) in real time can keep staff engaged. A low-cost approach is to use a netbook or Raspberry Pi computer attached to a display monitor. £250 outlay.

I have also used this approach of listing hyperlinks to provide an index of resources that are used a lot within a company. For example, there are some useful pages for finding IP addresses, looking up postcodes or checking companies.

Also, it is possible to produce sub-pages, so you could have an additional one for each department and use this approach to show specific information. One page could actually be the company information document that was described earlier. A DN document need not be a document in a repository; it could be a page on the dashboard. Equally, I have found a page devoted to the company's website can be useful, as it can log the versions of software, codes and styles being used, so that it acts as a crib sheet when things are updated or migrated in future.

Future proofing

Making it a policy that all key services are accessed from a central page ensures that everyone has visibility of the services in use, even if they do not have access to their function. If someone leaves a job, the services they may have used are there for others to gain access to. For example, marketing may have started a corporate Pinterest account, and few would know unless it appears on the dashboard.

At the end of the day, it is useful to have an internal home page for your company that is a first port of call for everyone to use in the company. This means it can also act as a bulletin board with messages posted or announcements made; and one tip is to make this the default homepage for the staff web browsers.

Third-party business software

There are plenty of software packages that help teams work together and run projects. Examples include Slack and Basecamp. These applications could form the basis of a dashboard as well, as certain pages can be set to show resources or web links with read-only properties.

Using a web-based intranet is also a good way to display and disseminate risk assessments, policies and, indeed, the entire staff handbook. Although the controlled document DN system can be retained to keep a handle on issue numbers and any changes, this approach can help make these documents more accessible. Links can also be provided to your own company server to allow the original or pdf copies to be downloaded.

Every company will have different metrics to monitor, different services in use and a different mindset amongst staff as how to best access information. However, usually a system gets adopted and stays in use when it is intuitive, requires little extra effort and everyone buys in to it because it becomes the way things are done.

At the time of exit, a dashboard can help the new owners take control of the business more quickly as well as help them integrate everything into their own existing systems. You will want the exit process to be smooth and require as simple a handover as possible, mainly so that you are locked in for less time. The dashboard will go a long way towards achieving this goal.

Take-away and to-do list

- Keeping an eye on all the services and devices being used by a company can be problematic. A central control panel or dashboard can be a useful way to provide links to them all, and encourages staff to have a 'go-to' place from which to access the company assets they use. As a director, you will have a bird's eye view and the ability to dip into any of the services as required.

☐ Create a simple webpage dashboard of links to key services.

☐ Add other pages to this intranet facility to enable some controlled documents in the DN system to be viewed by staff (eg, the staff handbook).

☐ Further functionality can be added to the dashboard by web developers or using the widgets on the platform selected.

22.

SCALE-UP

Corporate adolescence

As businesses and organizations grow they become complicated unwieldy beasts straddling territories and coping with different cultures. They are comprised of an army of individuals each with their own skills, desires, shortcomings and agendas. Unlike a colony of ants, these human resources are freethinking, often ambitious individuals with their own opinions. Some will even have an entrepreneurial spirit and just be biding their time before they make their own leap.

Anyone who has worked in a large organization, be it a multinational company, a government department or an academic institution, will know that there tends to be a debilitating layer of bureaucracy and damaging air of politics. Although it may sound pessimistic, without care, your enterprise can evolve into this state as well.

As your business grows, extra layers of management become necessary as people will need to be directed from above, and operational information will need to rise back up to the top. Even if you, as a founder, are determined to have a flat structure with plenty of delegated responsibility, these communication issues will still come about where your business spans geographical locations and time zones.

Exit warrant

During the scale-up phase, it becomes easier to lose sight of matters that will concern a future investor or acquirer. Larger businesses can have a growing number of skeletons in the cupboard that have either been forgotten, ignored or hidden without the management team knowing. Therefore it becomes more difficult for a detailed due diligence to be performed by a third party. It is also a lot more onerous for you as a director to sign on the dotted lines and warrant that all is in order; not just in the head office, but also in the production line down the road, the sales office overseas and the agent in the far corner of China. If you are growing rapidly, keep in mind that the process needs to be orderly for this reason.

Growing pains within a business also bring about other challenges. It is difficult for a company to remain agile and innovative as it becomes larger. The original core team gets dispersed more thinly and the initial culture of the organization becomes diluted. There is so much toing and froing trying to direct progress across departments and down the hierarchy of the team that cogs seem to grind and frustrations can build.

It is because of these changes in the evolving business that many start-up entrepreneurs find the growth stage unpalatable. Sometimes it is better to have someone else with a different temperament come on board and take the helm during the scale-up phase. Indeed, the board and investors may insist on this change of guard, so life can certainly alter for the original founders.

Scalable software systems

The key to the controlled growth of a business, I believe, is to have systems in place that scale with the organization. As you become a large organization with many customers, you will probably need to use an enterprise resource planning (ERP) system that pulls together processes within your various departments. This software will facilitate the management of customers, projects, production and staff.

One of the biggest costs of introducing an ERP system is breaking down and analyzing all the existing processes that have formed over time, and ensuring all the staff buy into the new system. If you have been systemizing your business from the outset, this implementation task becomes far easier. Much of the thinking outlined in this book should be easily incorporated into an ERP system: your financial systems, your marketing procedures, your sales processes and so on. All the ERP system does is bring it all together as a series of integrated software modules on a platform, arranged around the departments or functions that you already have in place in your business.

There are expensive corporate ERP systems aimed at the large multinationals provided by the likes of SAP, Oracle and IBM. However, there are also lower cost systems including those built on open source software such as OpenERP (now called Odoo). These variants can be free or inexpensive, depending on the level of functionality and number of users you intend to deploy. This means that you can introduce an ERP system into your fledgling company with little cost from the beginning. The advantage is that doing so will help you and your management team keep on top of things as you grow.

Social responsibility

A growing company also has to deal with more arduous responsibilities that are seemingly detached from your core business. For example, your business will start to be seen by outsiders as a key pillar of the community that you are operating in. Corporate social responsibility (CSR) will appear on the agenda; you may need to mentor smaller companies, support local charities, participate in local fundraising events, influence local policy on housing and skills (because your growing company is dependent on them), and consider issues around environmental impact of production, waste and traffic.

Your early engagement in the local community as a start-up will help your role develop as you grow. As a founder, I think it is beneficial to make time to be involved in the local business and community scene. Doing so will help you understand the concerns of local stakeholders, making sure that the growth of your business is not one of them.

Export

Most governments encourage their homegrown businesses to 'hurry up' and export overseas. To do so is actually a significant undertaking for a business, so although it may be inevitable, exporting products and services is a leap that should not be taken lightly.

There is plenty of government assistance to introduce you to contacts in foreign markets, but possibly the best advice will come from a company already selling there. Make this your mission before selling overseas; talk to another entrepreneur or business leader that already has experience doing it. They will have witnessed pitfalls, and unless they are your competitor, they will almost certainly offer advice to help you. They may even have staff and premises in place that you could utilize.

One experience that surprised me was just how many small companies in Singapore faced challenges operating in China. It was only a few years ago as China started to grow into a major manufacturing powerhouse of higher end goods such as electronics and computer hardware. Many Singaporeans speak both English and Chinese (some speak English and Malay, some English and Tamil, depending on their ethnic origin). Also, Singapore has a very strong Chinese culture. Yet they had real difficulty succeeding commercially in China, because business was done so differently. The analogy would be like British doing business in America; even if the culture is on the face of it similar, we all know that there are differences in approach.

Invaluable capex

It is well worth buying a few books for the library on the culture in new countries in which you are about to do business. The *Culture Shock* series is a good start. £15 per book outlay

---

Exporting products and services also brings with it complexities around legal compliance, tax (such as VAT), export licences and import duties. In such cases, there really is no substitute to paying for good advice from lawyers, tax accountants and informed authorities. However, from experience, money can be saved by undertaking a bit of research first to try to understand where your business will need extra help and advice.

To compound matters when you become an exporter, overseas customers can be less willing to paying on time and exchange rate fluctuations can create real problems in financial forecasting. You will be investing overseas one minute and then collecting payments the next, all whilst trying to pay for people and goods in a foreign currency.

Overseas agents

To help grow your export business, you could consider engaging an overseas sales agent or distributor. They are their own legal entities, separate from your business, and may already be undertaking this service for many companies. They should, therefore, be familiar with the local laws and culture and, ideally, understand the sector in which you wish to operate. You will need to do your homework to establish that they have a sound trading history and a good reputation in the industry.

Your business will contract an agent on a certain set of agreed terms and conditions concerning the price, specification and warranty of your products and services to be sold in the chosen territory. The agent will then be responsible for all the operations in the field and much of the legal compliance this brings with it.

You will want to be sure that your authorized agents adhere to your branding guidelines, your sales literature, your company ethos and so forth. It would be wise to include a provision around the length of time they will act on your behalf and what targets they will achieve in the territory. One day you may want to enter the country with a subsidiary, but equally if they do a good job, you will want them incentivized to continue.

Typical clauses in a contract of this nature will include whether or not they are an exclusive distributor for a territory, and what it is they will sell both for you and for others. Define this aspect of the contract clearly; is the territory a country or a region? and is the product or service everything you make or one product or indeed one version? Consider what happens if sales come through your main company website as well, and how any service element will be handled (like repair, maintenance or upgrade).

Milestones are important too. If an overseas agent is responsible for sales in a region, make sure they have clearly defined targets to reach. These goals could be based on volume or revenue, increasing year on year with termination clauses if the expected levels are not achieved. Equally, the agent will almost certainly insist on support from you and your team, so ensure you can provide it so that you are not the reason sales fail.

Think through what information an agent would benefit from and ideally give them limited access to your resources that have already been created. In general, overseas agents will need access like any other sales employee to your product literature, price lists, specifications and so forth. Therefore, use the file-sharing system on your server to provide appropriate access to the resources, and when documents are updated or changed, everyone sees the same version whether an employee or an agent.

Monitoring progress overseas is also critically important. Monthly reporting now needs to include figures from these new target territories, and that is not just sales figures, but stock levels, warranty issues, outstanding invoices, website analytics, social networking reach within this territory and so on.

Overseas subsidiaries

My experience with international growth was when Singular ID won Nanochallenge, an international competition for business plans in northern Italy. Peter and I had entered on a whim. Before we knew it, we had competed in Padua and won a €300,000 prize to set up in the Veneto region.

Strategically it made sense for us, as we wanted a European presence and northern Italy has a varied manufacturing industry that was relevant to our business. We went ahead and set up a subsidiary from Singapore and suddenly had to think about incorporation, accounting, recruitment, premises and sales in a new region with its own laws, culture, and language.

Remember too that each overseas subsidiary is a legal entity in its own right. It is like a start-up with the parent company as a backer. As such, you as a founder of the parent are likely to be a company director of the subsidiary as well, bringing with it more onerous responsibilities in a foreign country.

Straddling time zones can have advantages and disadvantages. If you have businesses in Asia, UK/Europe and the US, then those in the UK will have their work cut out communicating. Calls will start with Asia in the morning before colleagues finish for the day in the east, then it will be teleconferencing with the Americans to the west as they wake up late morning or late afternoon depending on which side of the country they are.

If you are organized, it means your business is active 24 hours a day with the baton being handed over from Asia to Europe to the US and back to Asia. If you are disorganized, then expensive operations can abruptly stop until you answer your phone at 4am in the morning or 11pm at night.

Doing business overseas involves a lot of travel, a lot of learning and a great deal of anxiety. It sounds cool to say that you have just opened your office in New York, Dubai or Tokyo, but make sure there is a sound business case for doing so and remember that each office will be like a start-up all over again; everything I have talked about in this book will apply on the ground from the outset because they will be a microcosm of your enlarged business.

Joint ventures

With growth may come joint ventures (JV) where you create subsidiaries of shared ownership in other sectors or other territories. A JV is again another legal entity with initially a start-up profile; you will need to go back to the beginning of this book and run through all the tasks and considerations for the JV entity. And being a jointly owned start-up, it will need the other party to buy into the methods and processes you bring along whilst being mindful they have their own systems and processes which they may want to use in the new entity. As you can imagine, a JV brings a complexity usually reserved for larger companies.

In Singular ID, we nearly started a JV in the automotive sector. The idea was to team up with another company who had the domain knowledge and we would supply the technology. During the preparation phase, it became apparent how complex the arrangement might be. Firstly, the new entity had to have a share structure, a governance process, and then a full business plan and strategy detached from both parent companies. The exercise was instructive because it brought into sharp relief the amount of extra work that would be required for both parties in operating the JV. In effect, the JV is like a marriage with plenty of prenuptials and the need for a long-term commitment. In the end, we did not proceed, largely because our acquisition changed the priorities for both parties.

Cross-border documentation control

For simplicity and efficiency, you will want the new overseas agent, the country manager in the overseas subsidiary or the JV company to use your existing documents and templates whenever possible. They will almost certainly need modifying at a local level; possibly to change the language, possibly to comply with local law and possibly to fit with the local culture or market. Therefore, you will want document control to cascade down from the head office. If you change a policy, a price or a specification, it will need to be reflected in their documentation as quickly as possible. This requirement applies to staff documents, commercial contracts and marketing material.

Following the incorporation of Singular ID Italia, we had a capable country manager, Stefano, come onboard, who embraced our document scheme and replicated much of what we had in Italian. This saved him time, as he did not have to reinvent the wheel, but it also helped our group of companies because we knew policies and literature were aligned.

One way to achieve this document control is why we ensured the DN system included details of the country or territory as well. So, we used the MyCo-GB- prefixes for the documents in a UK company and would use MyCo-US- for a case in the US.

You will also need to put in place a table or chart that maps equivalent documents. Even if US versions are created in parallel with UK versions with equivalent numbers, it will not happen all the time and so cannot be relied upon. As such, a table needs to be created saying which ones map across to which ones, so that if either are updated (in particular the originating one), changes are made throughout.

Remember the country code refers to the location of the legal entity, not the fact that you may have several offices in a country. Therefore, you can have a New York and Los Angeles office all being part of MyCompany Inc and all using the one set of documents based on the MyCo-US- system. The complexity with the US example is that state laws may require separate documents to exist for each of the US states in which the company operates.

This need for international document control may be sounding like a bureaucratic nightmare, but believe me when I say the other alternative is an altogether bigger nightmare wherein all subsidiaries have their own system and create their own documents without recourse to the parent company. This situation can end up with the company in a right pickle, be it legal or financial.

Financial pressures

The real challenges with scale-up are around managing cashflow whilst coping with multiple business locations and different currencies. Cashflow problems arise from an ever-expanding customer base preceded by an increasing number of staff and investment in facilities to generate this growth.

In the end, you will win or lose financially by being organized with your operations and adept at forecasting your costs and sales. The good news is that this forecasting is all down to you and your team, so getting clear channels of communication in place so that everyone can contribute to the picture will help.

Adapting to seize opportunities

Larger companies with a solid trading history have the advantage that they may be able to secure bigger contracts and have more sway in negotiations, but equally they bring with them the baggage of earlier years.

Growth can also bring with it other opportunities. As your product, service, technology and enterprise matures, you may find that you need to quickly change business model to cope. For example, you may go from manufacturing in-house on a small scale to using toll-manufacturing services in the Far East. You may also find that you start licensing your own IP much more widely, having to support customers around the world and investing in your technology and associated processes.

However, as a founder, if you have completed the groundwork for your business and been able to delegate tasks successfully during the start-up stage, so the scale-up phase can often progress more smoothly. Having the culture and processes embedded in the fabric of the business is akin to having the company's DNA dispersed throughout its operations home and abroad.

As you grow, so too you are more likely to encounter disputes; be they employment disputes, product liability issues or even IP litigation. Having all your records and processes in place from early on will help you deal with these issues and put them to bed that much more quickly.

Ultimately, the growth of a business from local start-up to international scale-up can be exciting and mind expanding, but your key to ongoing success will be a capable forward-looking team, well-oiled processes and good-quality information on which to act. As a founder, your challenge will be to have enough free-thinking time to formulate and execute the growth strategy without being the pivot that everyone comes to for decisions and actions.

A growing business with an international footprint will certainly appeal to an acquirer that wants to build their own global presence or can see synergies with your operations and theirs. However, as you scale, beware that you could become too large for a prospective suitor to swallow. Therefore, despite the value of your business increasing, an exit through trade sale may in fact become harder to achieve, as there will be fewer businesses that could afford to buy you. It should not be a reason to stall growth, but is worth keeping in mind as you review your exit plan.

Take-away and to-do list

- Scaling up involves all that has gone before many times over again. Each overseas agent, subsidiary or joint venture will require many or indeed all of the structures and processes you have developed. Growth can be expensive and daunting, but equally it can be the kink in the hockey-stick curve where you suddenly take off. In reality, scaling up is what happens after you reach the summit of the first incline of a rollercoaster; it has required untold effort to drag yourself to that peak and suddenly you lurch into even more unknowns at pace.

☐ Roll out overseas controlled documents using the MyCo-CC-DNxxxx.y system where CC is now the next country in question.

☐ Map the various documents so that different country versions can stay in step as iterations are made.

☐ Do not rush exports – always talk to a few local businesses in the overseas location first to understand the lie of the land.

23.

VENTURE OR VULTURE CAPITALISTS?

Approaching rounds of finance

Raising money to fund your business can be a stressful and disheartening affair. Generally speaking, when you need money, there is an urgency to secure it in record time before the existing money in the bank runs out and before you are compelled to stop trading. Unfortunately, raising money takes a lot longer to complete than you expect, and the circling investors know your desperation is heightening and that if they drag out the process for long enough they can swoop in and get a better (cheaper) deal.

The key here is to be poker face and organized. If you can start preparing the groundwork early enough and be well prepared, the due diligence will be shorter and less time consuming for you. If you can begin well before the panic sets in, you can turn the tables and start a feeding frenzy in which multiple investors are competing to take a stake in your business. And finally, if you stay in control, you can walk away from a poor offer rather than being compelled to accept one at a time of desperation.

If your business is likely to need investment in the future, you can prepare the ground from the outset. Start to identify venture capitalists in your territory and market sector: make a point of meeting them at events, chatting to them informally and letting them know about your business opportunity.

Then, add their contact details to your newsletter mailing list so that they see you making progress before they are part of the story. One of their biggest risks is understanding the subtleties of a business and the people behind it. If they start to get to know you and see your team making progress they will not only see your capability, they will start wishing they had a stake in your business too.

Then, when it comes to negotiating the investment deal, keep a few things in mind.

The investor's mindset

Firstly, you will need to work closely with this organization as you move forward. They will be climbing into bed with you as a shareholder and quite likely becoming a director. Be aware that the representative you are dealing with beforehand may not be the person you end up with. They could move on or they may be the deal-seeker not the subsequent partner. You will need to be sure that you can work with their organization's culture and within their timeframes.

Most investors have a timeline when they want their money back, often tied to the particular investment fund's lifetime, so be aware if it is a horizon of one, three or five years and understand what happens when this is reached.

Talk with the founders and CEOs of other investee companies to see how well it has been going. Are the investors hands on, do they oust the management team soon after investment, do they bring useful contacts, are they report heavy and do they honour their side of the bargain with timely investments when milestones are met?

Then you need to beware of the tricks the sophisticated venture capitalist and investor can pull. They have likely been investing in businesses for a long time and seen many companies; you are probably on your first business struggling to keep it going and have little experience of the process.

Their sole aim is to make money and protect their position. Whatever they say, they are not going to be charitable or take any unnecessary risks. By and large, they are investing other people's money and being paid a sizeable fee to return it with gains. As such, they will not want you to have too much control nor for you to make any financial gains before they do.

Investment agreements

This is where a host of protective provisions come in. Your company's memorandum of articles of association, shareholders' agreement and investment agreement will start to bulge with new clauses.

Keep a close eye on these additional terms as they are drafted and try to understand their ramifications for different business scenarios. Use your budget, your forecasts and your capitalization table to asses quantitatively what these provisions will mean in different scenarios.

Exit warrant

Your warrants are signed in blood when a new, sophisticated investor comes on board. Always take legal advice and always read what you are signing up for. Remember that another investment or acquisition deal may follow in the future, so do not throw the baby out with the bathwater at this stage.

Here are some more clauses that are likely to occur where investors are concerned.

Future-price floor

Investors will likely set a limit for how low a share price the company can be sold for. You may have put in a lot of time and effort but not so much real cash. They will be putting in real cash and do not want to be short changed. Generally, this provision is reasonable, but watch what the level is; often it is set as a multiple of their investment. If they invested at £10 per share, they may set a lower boundary of £20 per share because they not only want to avoid losing money, they also want to make it (double at a minimum). The question is what if an offer is made for £15 per share in the short term. Everyone would actually make quite a bit of money and yet you would not be in a position to sell.

Preference shares

Investors will often impose limits of control on what shareholders can vote on and how many votes are needed. A simple way for them to achieve this is to create preference shares which are a different class of shares from ordinary shares, that have certain preferences attached to them. You need to watch this aspect carefully, as some of these preferences could be quite significant.

If they are to be the only holders of such class of shares (and they will almost certainly stipulate no more such shares can be issued without their permission), they may well have full control over certain matters. For example, the sale of the company may only be possible if agreed by the preference shareholders. This provision could be paraphrased as: 'if we the investor don't want to sell, whatever the deal, you can't'.

Remember that they will generally be motivated by one of two things: greed and the timeline of their funds. They may not want to sell when you do despite a good price, simply because they have a few more years to run on their fund and they think they could sell for even more later. Or they may want to sell fairly quickly to a lower offer because their fund needs to liquidate. Either way, you could be at their beck and call if they have veto rights. Therefore, try to ensure that they cannot veto a deal that is otherwise reasonable for the shareholders.

Tag-along rights

The term 'tag-along' is a right that if any of the company's shares are sold, the party to which tag-along applies have a right to sell as well. This provision will primarily prevent you and any other founders from selling your shares without the others selling theirs at the same time for the same price. This process stops you making money and leaving the business whilst the remaining shareholders are left in a business without the key players.

This consideration is not a bad provision, but it should apply to all shareholders including the investors and other minority shareholders. Basically, if an offer is made to buy shares, everyone can participate and tag along. Participating is generally an option, so you do not have to go along and sell your shares with the others if you do not want to. Sometimes this is set out as a proportional option as well; if a shareholder has the opportunity to sell half their shareholding, so too can the others with their tag-along rights.

Drag-along rights

Drag-along rights provide a flip side to the tag-along clause. This provision insists that if a shareholder has a valid offer for shares, every other shareholder is compelled to accept this offer too. This prevents shareholders, either majority or minority stakeholders, jeopardizing a merger or acquisition.

For example, if you as a founder are offered £50 per share for the entire company and one shareholder decides that for whatever reason this is not of interest, the deal could be blown. As long as the other provisions, such as a minimum price are met, then these additional rights compel a shareholder to be dragged along with the rest of them.

Anti-dilution rights

Anti-dilution is another interesting provision, as this clause protects the size or proportion of a shareholder's stake in the company. The provision can take a variety of forms, but in its simplest form it gives a shareholder the right to maintain the proportion of its stake in the company and to buy more shares at the new (hopefully higher) share price at the same time as a new or future investor.

This provision is of interest because it allows an investor to maintain a consistent stake in the company that in turn could provide more returns in the future. When exercising an anti-dilution right like this, it suggests that the value of the company is increasing because shares are being bought by multiple parties at a new higher price.

The provision may also be tied with some other clauses; keeping a certain-sized shareholding might be enough to influence a future decision during a vote. For example, if another provision says that whilst holding 20% or more shares the organization is able to elect a representative to the Board, then an anti-dilution provision may keep this right in place.

Exercising an anti-dilution provision of this nature is generally a good thing as it means existing investors are still on board and optimistic about the future. They would be unlikely to invest more money if they thought otherwise. Also, if you can establish which investors are likely to exercise such a right during a round of finance, you can include this money as part of the investment round and perhaps raise less from another investor. The right also helps with attracting a new investor, because if exercised it shows that others are still prepared to put in new money as well.

The anti-dilution provisions you have to watch are those where they are automatic or at a discounted share price. If an investor expects a provision in which new shares are issued at par value or at the original price, these can damage a company's share structure and often lead to the founders being severely diluted.

Sometimes the mistake is made that everyone can have an anti-dilution provision (including the founders). If everyone has the right, then no new investors would be able to put in money as everyone else could exercise their right and you would go around in circles trying to maintain everyone's share proportion of the company. Therefore, founders don't generally get given the right (and they are usually the ones least likely to be able to afford it anyway, otherwise why have third party investors).

Evergreen anti-dilution is also a clause to watch. Early investors or groups providing a service like office space in lieu of equity, may say they want to maintain a small stake (like 1% or 5%) of the business in perpetuity and for these shares to be issued without them stumping up any cash (other than perhaps the par value of the share, eg, £1 per share).

These deals may sound like a good way to save money at the outset, but for a business that grows well, the value of these small holdings could be very high and disproportionate. Also, what happens if you no longer need these services from the accountant or facility; make sure they do not keep being issued new shares.

Pre-emption rights

A pre-emption right is on the face of it similar to an anti-dilution right; it is the right to buy shares before another party and is often applied to publicly listed companies so that institutional investors have the right to buy more shares ahead of an offer to the general public.

The difference with a pre-emption right is that it could allow an investor to buy more shares than their current stake, ie, they could increase their holding and their influence. This can be a good thing in that they may want to invest more at a particular price and save you the time in seeking a new investor. But beware of the consequences on the capitalization table and how strong their voting position will be in the future; it is much akin to a hostile takeover.

Put option

Where sophisticated investors have a timeline to meet, they will often insist on a 'put option'. This is a provision that will allow them, at their discretion, to sell their shares at a particular price in the future.

For example, an investor may say I have the right to sell at £1 a share to any buyer between three and four years from now (when their fund needs to liquidate). This is a provision that will allow them to extract some money for their shares (probably way less than they paid) to release them from your company and in effect write off the investment. You need to watch this provision because it could allow someone else to take a sizable stake at little cost in your company. Make sure that existing shareholders have a first right of refusal, perhaps the founders foremost. Also, ensure that the put option does not then invoke all the drag-along and tag-along provisions too; you do not want to be compelled to sell at this price, and nor do you want others to have the option to sell short, get out and leave you with more unknowns.

Call option

The opposite of a put option is a call option. Sometimes investors will try to sneak in some provision to get more upside in the future. They may impose a call option that they can exercise at their discretion to buy more shares at some point in the future at a predetermined price. They will only tend to exercise this right if things are going well, which could artificially depress your share price at the next round of investment.

For example, you might be gunning for an investment at £150 per share and a call option is in existence that enables the investor to buy a number of shares at £100. The new investor will use this lower price as a bargaining tool to lower their investment price; the existing investor with the call option will be keen to exercise the right and secure a bargain.

A down-round

Ultimately, bringing on board a sophisticated third-party investor should be a good thing, and if they come with lots of provisions to shaft you, you can rightly ask if they might be the best investors to attract.

Things tend to only turn nasty when the company is not doing so well; milestones may be missed, sales may be down, progress may be slow. In this situation, you need everyone to come together and fight for a common cause rather than them invoke nasty clauses in investment agreements.

The result, however, can be a down-round in which more money is taken on at a lower share price than last time. The event can be demoralizing for all concerned, even though it is a better situation than winding the whole company up and the share price being effectively zero.

This situation is illustrated in Table 23.1 in which another round of investment has had to be made by another investor (VC2) in which the share price fell from £20 previously to £18 this time.

Investment round	Share-holder	Number of shares	Price per share	This investment	Investment to date	Post-money valuation	Owner-ship
0: incorp	Founder 1	10,000	£1.00	£10,000	£10,000	£10,000	50%
	Founder 2	10,000	£1.00	£10,000	£10,000	£10,000	50%
	Total	*20,000*	*£1.00*	*£20,000*	*£20,000*	*£20,000*	*100%*
1: f&f	Founder 1	10,000	£2.00	-	£10,000	£20,000	44.5%
	Founder 2	10,000	£2.00	-	£10,000	£20,000	44.5%
	Friend 1	2,500	£2.00	£5,000	£5,000	£5,000	11%
	Total	*22,500*	*£2.00*	*£5,000*	*£25,000*	*£45,000*	*100%*
2: angel	Founder 1	10,000	£5.00	-	£10,000	£50,000	38%
	Founder 2	10,000	£5.00	-	£10,000	£50,000	38%
	Friend 1	2,500	£5.00	-	£5,000	£12,500	9%
	Angel 1	4,000	£5.00	£20,000	£20,000	£20,000	15%
	Total	*26,500*	*£5.00*	*£20,000*	*£45,000*	*£132,500*	*100%*
3: early VC	Founder 1	10,000	£20.00	-	£10,000	£200,000	28%
	Founder 2	10,000	£20.00	-	£10,000	£200,000	28%
	Friend 1	2,500	£20.00	-	£5,000	£50,000	7%
	Angel 1	4,000	£20.00	-	£20,000	£80,000	11%
	VC 1	7,000	£20.00	£140,000	£140,000	£140,000	20%
	ESOP	2,000	£20.00	-	£0	£40,000	6%
	Total	*35,500*	*£20.00*	*£140,000*	*£185,000*	*£710,000*	*100%*
4: main VC	Founder 1	10,000	£18.00	-	£10,000	£180,000	16.5%
	Founder 2	10,000	£18.00	-	£10,000	£180,000	16.5%
	Friend 1	2,500	£18.00	-	£5,000	£45,000	4%
	Angel 1	4,000	£18.00	-	£20,000	£72,000	7%
	VC 1	12,000	£18.00	-	£140,000	£216,000	20%
	ESOP	2,000	£18.00	-	£0	£36,000	3%
	VC 2	20,000	£18.00	£360,000	£360,000	£360,000	33%
	Total	*60,500*	*£18.00*	*£360,000*	*£545,000*	*£1,089,000*	*100%*

Table 23.1. An illustrative capitalization table of a down-round.

This situation may have come about through hard negotiation up to the wire, so the outcome kept the company trading and brought in much needed working capital. However, several things are of note:

The new investor has invested a sizable chunk of money, £360,000, which may well be needed to keep the company running a sensible amount of time or to get it through an impending cashflow problem. This has resulted in the new investor (or consortium) owning 33% of the company.

Furthermore, it will be noted that VC1 has increased its shareholding from 7,000 to 12,000 shares and yet the table indicates that no further money was invested from this party. This illustrates the power (and danger) of protective provisions. In this case VC1 had an anti-dilution clause that stated in the event of a down-round in which shares were issued at a lower price than their investment round (ie, £20), they will be issued with free new shares so that they retain the same proportion of share ownership, ie, 20%. In order to achieve this, the company had to issue 5,000 new shares and this nearly doubled their holding. This issuance, of course, was at the expense of everyone else; the founders having taken a big hit in which they have lost majority control of their company and between them have the same voting proportion as the new investor (33%).

This example highlights the importance of a capitalization table, as it shows the effect of an investment (hopefully before it is agreed upon) and can indicate where power struggles may lie in future shareholder votes.

The post-money valuation of the company after this round is now over a million pounds, but the founders' and early investors' shareholding value is reduced because the share price has fallen and their stake has remained the same.

The value of VC1's holding has had an interesting turn, however. It has retained the same proportion of a company with a higher value, so although the share price fell, the value of its shareholding has increased significantly to £216,000 from £140,000. This just goes to show how a simple innocuous sounding provision agreed upon in the past can have a serious impact in the future.

Moreover, VC1 could well have liaised with VC2 and encouraged the slight down-round as it was in their interest to promote it; it helped bring on VC2 to share the risk and they ended up with more shares and more value. A fairer provision for the Founders would be an agreement that issues new shares, so that the value of VC1's shareholding is maintained after the down-round not the proportion of the shareholding. This scenario would have involved issuing just under 780 new shares to VC1, so significantly less than the 5,000 described. The devil is in the detail, so always try to model future scenarios with the capitalization table.

The fact that 'the value of your investment may go up or down and there is no guarantee that you will get back what you have put in' is never truer in a start-up where you are the founder. Lots of things can go wrong in this high-risk environment, so being organized and on top of the situation when raising finance can help enormously. The aim should be to secure timely up-rounds, however small the increment in share price turns out to be, so that everyone remains motivated and the trend for the business is positive.

Take-away and to-do list

- Be prepared to negotiate hard with a future investor and make it a beauty parade in which they are being judged. This can only be done if you have time and a compelling story, so pace yourself with the fundraising. Watch the clauses being introduced into an investment agreement by a sophisticated investor like a hawk.

☐ Use the capitalization table to simulate investment-round scenarios.

☐ Build a list of potential investors and engage with them well before you need them.

☐ Work through and agree on a term sheet with respect to an investment agreement before embarking on the costly and time-consuming work of drafting a full agreement.

24.

A SHARP EXIT

Towards an acquisition

When my co-founder and I started our business together in Singapore, our aim from the outset was to position the business to sell. We were both in a foreign country, so although we liked the Singapore lifestyle, we were not in the mindset of settling there for good, nor indeed for starting a business that would create a job for life. Our plan was to build a technology business, secure some early sales, and then sell the business to a larger player. Remarkably the plans came together and we were able to exit in a time frame of about two-and-half years from incorporation.

One of things that made it easier was being prepared and making sure the business was in a fit state to sell. We were actually approached by four companies interested in purchasing the business over that short period of time. Three were particularly serious and did a fair amount of due diligence. One saw it through and closed the deal.

Just like raising venture capital, selling a business is equally draining on the resources of the business. Firstly, the management team needs to meet with the prospective acquirers and service their every enquiry. Therefore, just as with having everything ready for an investor, so to it helps to have the documents and reports on hand for a suitor.

Secrecy can also be a problem, particularly if you are negotiating with a listed company; these kinds of transactions can be highly market sensitive. So it is often necessary to keep everything on a need-to-know basis and only allow some staff to know the real nature of all the meetings. One way is to explain the visits as being related to a future potential investment or collaboration and leave it as that.

Exit warrant

This is what it is all been building towards: a warrant at the time of exit that boils down to saying the business being sold is inside what it says on the tin. Highlight the positives and faults honestly, and you will be able to sleep easily when the cheque arrives.

Many of the negotiations will be similar in nature to those with investors. The difference, of course, is that you are selling all of the shares rather than issuing new ones. The result will be relinquishing control of the business and hopefully receiving well-deserved cash for your shares to reward you for all your hard work in building the business.

The terms of a trade sale

Things to watch at this stage are that it really is a cash transaction. Many larger companies may suggest paying for your shares with their company shares. This is cheap for them in that they can just issue more and take a hit on the share price rather than having to find real cash. However, shares can go up or down, and so the number you will be paid for in shares at a certain price may well go down (or up) in the future. Bear in mind that the price change may be immediate, as once the transaction is made public in the case of a listed company, the markets will respond to the deal and the swing of the share price may not be favourable.

The share price is one thing to consider, but then there is the issue of how liquid their shares are; can you sell them if you want to? or are they traded so infrequently that you will not be able to rid yourselves of them for many years? Listed companies tend to have more liquidity, but even that depends on the stock market they are listed on and how fashionable the sector you are operating in is.

Some good arguments to use during a negotiation are that you need cash to spread your risk. You do not want to realize your investment and be issued with shares in one single company over which you will have little control. That way you might be able to have a mix of cash and shares.

Also, if you are going to take shares, use your experience from dealing with investors, as in effect that is what you are now becoming. Firstly, you should ask for more shares in terms of value than cash because the risk is so much higher. Then you should look at some of the conditions, such as a right to sell them back to the company at a particular price should the market rate fall below this. This is a put option. You could also demand some preferences in terms of dividend payments, anti-dilution and so forth to protect your position.

As you can see, this is starting to become complicated, and if you keep pushing this, they may well see the benefits of an all-cash deal too.

You also need to be aware of tax legislation. If you sell your shares for shares, you will still almost certainly need to pay a personal capital gains tax and for this you'll need cash. Having all your gains tied up in shares that you are unable to sell could cause you cashflow problems personally. Again, use this as a bargaining tool to ensure as much of the deal as possible is in cash.

The acquirer's mindset

When an acquirer is looking to buy your business, they will also be concerned that everything is as it seems, and more importantly they'll want some of the key personnel (usually the founders or directors) to be compelled to stay on. They will also want the core management team to stay motivated and continue operating the business whilst it is gradually integrated in to their operations.

This 'lock-in' or 'tie-in' is not unusual. As a founder, you have to be mentally prepared for this period. Firstly, you will have to work for some time under new management. The new owners may well say you will stay in charge, but it is unlikely; the new company will almost certainly want to introduce their ethos, their processes, their branding or their strategy on what was once yours and is now their business. Therefore, make sure you can cope with the negotiated time frames; is it a six-month handover? a year lock-in? or a two-year purgatory? The length of time is often higher for technology businesses where there is a lot of know-how and expertise in the founders' brains that will need extracting.

Over this period, ensure that you will be paid a salary. Prior to exit is the time to negotiate a higher salary because you will be compelled to work. During negotiations, try to add some performance-related bonuses, relating to what they want for the next stage of the business that will appease their own shareholders. Examples include sales bonuses, product-development bonuses and so on.

Sometimes the cash will be released in stages to the founders so that they do not become rich overnight and suddenly lose interest in running the business for the new owners. Although a sale price may be agreed and the third-party investors almost certainly paid off fully on completion of the deal, the founders may well receive an upfront sum and then further amounts at regular intervals such as every six months. Things to watch here are that the cash is not tied to anything in the future; you need that cash to sit in an escrow or trust account with a solicitor to be released against a simple set of rules (such as dates). This way, the cash will have been paid up and the ownership does not still reside with the acquirer who may have their own problems in the future unrelated to your transaction.

Just beware that there are of course tax implications for any structure. So you will need expert advice on all of the proposed arrangements. For example, you may be better to transfer your shares to a trust and not realize a capital gain until the actual cash is released at each stage. This way you will still have a gain, but it will be spread out when you can afford to pay the associated tax. The series of gains may also occur in later tax years when you could have some new annual allowances to offset. Equally, this may not align well with entrepreneur tax relief that may require you to sell all your holding in one go. So talk to a good tax accountant before signing any deals.

The other bargaining tool is that as a founder or director, you should command a fair amount of respect. After all, you have helped build the business that they are keen to acquire. As much as you may feel like a David up against a Goliath, they will want you to remain motivated, helpful, keen and eager going forward helping them keep everything on the rails.

Keep alluding to this fact if the suitors propose deals that are not so palatable. If the acquirers want to pay you less cash, say how you want to be in a position to pay off debts and mortgages that you had to take out over the years to fund the business. If they want to tie you in longer, explain that you will be keen to continue to work with them going forward, but that you work better with the freedom to make that choice rather than being compelled to do so by handcuffs, however golden they are.

Shareholder benefits

Table 24.1 illustrates the capitalization table at the time of an exit by a trade sale. It considers that the company manages to sell its entire share capital at a share price of £36.00.

Investment Round	Share-holder	Number of shares	Price per share	This investment	Investment to date	Post-money valuation	Owner-ship
0: incorp	Founder 1	10,000	£1.00	£10,000	£10,000	£10,000	50%
	Founder 2	10,000	£1.00	£10,000	£10,000	£10,000	50%
	Total	*20,000*	*£1.00*	*£20,000*	*£20,000*	*£20,000*	*100%*
1: f&f	Founder 1	10,000	£2.00	-	£10,000	£20,000	44.5%
	Founder 2	10,000	£2.00	-	£10,000	£20,000	44.5%
	Friend 1	2,500	£2.00	£5,000	£5,000	£5,000	11%
	Total	*22,500*	*£2.00*	*£5,000*	*£25,000*	*£45,000*	*100%*
2: angel	Founder 1	10,000	£5.00	-	£10,000	£50,000	38%
	Founder 2	10,000	£5.00	-	£10,000	£50,000	38%
	Friend 1	2,500	£5.00	-	£5,000	£12,500	9%
	Angel 1	4,000	£5.00	£20,000	£20,000	£20,000	15%
	Total	*26,500*	*£5.00*	*£20,000*	*£45,000*	*£132,500*	*100%*
3: early VC	Founder 1	10,000	£20.00	-	£10,000	£200,000	28%
	Founder 2	10,000	£20.00	-	£10,000	£200,000	28%
	Friend 1	2,500	£20.00	-	£5,000	£50,000	7%
	Angel 1	4,000	£20.00	-	£20,000	£80,000	11%
	VC 1	7,000	£20.00	£140,000	£140,000	£140,000	20%
	ESOP	2,000	£20.00	-	£0	£40,000	6%
	Total	*35,500*	*£20.00*	*£140,000*	*£185,000*	*£710,000*	*100%*
4: main VC	Founder 1	10,000	£18.00	-	£10,000	£180,000	16.5%
	Founder 2	10,000	£18.00	-	£10,000	£180,000	16.5%
	Friend 1	2,500	£18.00	-	£5,000	£45,000	4%
	Angel 1	4,000	£18.00	-	£20,000	£72,000	7%
	VC 1	12,000	£18.00	-	£140,000	£216,000	20%
	ESOP	2,000	£18.00	-	£0	£36,000	3%
	VC 2	20,000	£18.00	£360,000	£360,000	£360,000	33%
	Total	*60,500*	*£18.00*	*£360,000*	*£545,000*	*£1,089,000*	*100%*
Trade sale	Founder 1	10,000	£36.00	-	£10,000	£360,000	16.5%
	Founder 2	10,000	£36.00	-	£10,000	£360,000	16.5%
	Friend 1	2,500	£36.00	-	£5,000	£90,000	4%
	Angel 1	4,000	£36.00	-	£20,000	£144,000	7%
	VC 1	12,000	£36.00	-	£140,000	£432,000	20%
	ESOP	2,000	£36.00	-	£0	£72,000	3%
	VC 2	20,000	£36.00	-	£360,000	£720,000	33%
	Total	*60,500*	*£36.00*	*£0*	*£545,000*	*£2,178,000*	*100%*

Table 24.1. An example capitalization table at the point of exit.

In this example, all is well that ends well. The company is sold for just over £2m and the founders each make £360,000 after investing £10,000 cash at the start (and no doubt a lot of blood, sweat and tears in the interim). The friend makes a healthy return on her £5,000 investment, as indeed does the angel who invested a little later but still during the high-risk early days. Not surprisingly, VC1 has done very well because they were shrewd enough to have some favourable protective provisions at the time of a down-round, and receive nearly half a million in cash.

The members of the employee share option scheme (ESOP) can each now exercise their options. Their strike price may have been set at £20 when the share scheme was set up. With the share price now £36, the effect for them is that they can buy the shares at £20 and sell them straight away to the acquiring company at £36. Employees thus make £16 profit per share, possibly tax free if the scheme was set up and run properly.

Finally, VC2 doubled their money in the time they were invested, so will also be relatively happy with the outcome. Of course, this simple illustration is only an example. In reality, VCs are likely to invest more cash over several rounds and a VC-funded company is likely to be sold at a much higher valuation in the tens of millions of pounds at the end of it all.

In the press, you only tend to hear about the big deals, and much is made of 'unicorns' which are businesses valued at over £1bn (or $1bn). However, everything is relative, and this example serves to show how a small business could grow with investment and result in a modest but profitable outcome for all the stakeholders at exit.

Invaluable capex

Champagne all round.

Initial public offering

The trade sale is only one kind of exit. Another exit is to list on a stock market and is known as an initial public offering or IPO. The advantage of this approach is that you can sell some of your shares, and more in the future, whilst still potentially retaining control of your business and unlocking the ability to issue more shares and raise more finance from the public and institutional investors in the future.

The process of listing is, however, demanding on management time and also comes at a price. You'll need to engage a consultant to help prepare all the information for the prospectus and then you will need to head off on roadshows to market your business so that the IPO happens with a bang and institutional investors are poised to buy into your company. The preparations will be much the same as for attracting venture capitalists or trade sale acquirers.

Operating as a public company requires transparency, regular reporting, regulatory compliance and the ability to control aspects of the business so that there are no surprises or embarrassments. All of this activity needs to happen after the listing. Despite it being an exit, you will almost certainly still be there in command. Hence, if you have all the controls in place from the beginning, it will be business as usual and things should not dramatically change as you move forward.

For the founder that enjoys operating a larger company, the IPO can be a great exit route. The outcome is that some of the founder's shares are usually sold, but many remain invested to give the public investor confidence. Further sales of shares are then subject to insider dealing rules and disclosure.

Management buy-out

Other forms of exit for you as a founder could involve a management or family buy-out in which you sell your shares to one or more successors. This route is not unlike a trade sale, but tends to be a more private affair involving colleagues and relations. Many of the considerations discussed apply and you may well be retained as a consultant or mentor rather than being operationally active.

Once again, all the processes and procedures that we have discussed will help with the sale. Hopefully, the management buy-out players are fully bought into the set-up, using it day in day out, and understand that they can continue running the business without you at the helm.

No one expects the exit

If all goes well, then at some point you may suddenly find yourself out of a job, comfortably wealthy and without the pressures of the business bearing down on you.

This situation can feel liberating, but more likely somewhat daunting too. Did you really build that business? Should you really have sold when you did? Did you make enough money or were you short changed? Are your staff all okay or will they be suffering under the new regime? These concerns are all natural for the entrepreneur who started, built and exited a business which of course was the be-all and end-all of life during the hectic period of running the business.

Dealing with all of these concerns is actually a nice problem to have. The main thing is to celebrate the achievement and either retire gracefully or formulate a new plan. It is amazing how many successful entrepreneurs become serial entrepreneurs craving the excitement one more time. The good news is that you may have more money to act as a cushion the next time around. And you will certainly have masses of hindsight and valuable experiences to build on for the next installment. You will also be in a fantastic position to help other budding entrepreneurs and small business owners, which can be a good way to keep yourself busy if the garden starts to become oppressive.

Take-away and to-do list:

- Opportunities to exit a business are a bit like buses; there are none for ages and then suddenly many come along almost at once. This means you need to be prepared and patient, and know what you want out of the deal.

- ☐ Identify potential acquirers over time (competitors and businesses operating in parallel sectors or other territories).

- ☐ Treat an acquisition in the same way as an investment: agree a term sheet and take legal and financial advice.

- ☐ Use the capitalization table to plan scenarios and ensure all the shareholders' various protective provisions are accounted for in the transaction.

APPENDIX A

A SYSTEM FOR COMPANY DOCUMENTS

This table provides a detailed structure for the possible directories and folders within your company's server so as to mirror the functions of typical departments.

Examples of what might be contained in each directory are suggested. Although every business is different, if you set up a system along these lines and put the relevant documents in the right place, you will have a flexible and scalable system. Most importantly, it will be able to adapt and grow with your company and allow new staff to find the information they need based on their job function without too much fuss.

Top directory	Sub-directory	Typical contents
00-DOCS	00-ARCHIVE	Copies of old versions for reference.
	01-DN	Index file: 00-KIQ-DN Document Register. Documents: MyCo-CC-DN000x.y (latest versions)
	02-SA	Index file: 00-KIQ-SA Signed agreements register. Documents: MyCo-CC-SA000x (scanned signed versions, limited access permissions)

Top directory	Sub-directory	Typical contents
01-BRD	00-ARCHIVE	Old files for reference.
	01-INCORP	Memorandum and articles of association. Records: incorporation papers and resolutions.
	02-SHLDRS	Shareholder records. Shareholder agreements. AGMs, EGMs, reports, agendas, minutes.
	03-PAPERS	Board resolutions, reports, agendas, minutes.
	04-COY HSE	General Company House correspondence.
	05-HMRC	Top-level HMRC tax authority correspondence.
	06-BANK	Top-level banking correspondence.
	07-INS	Top-level insurance documents and records.
	08-H&S	Top-level health and safety records.
	09-BPLANS	Strategic planning.
	10-ISSUES	Other board level records, correspondence etc.
	11-INFO	Resources for the board such as articles, news and white papers. Wherever possible these should be placed in other department INFO directories so that relevant departments can benefit from them as well.
	Example contributions to 01-DN shared folder	Annual company report.

Top directory	Sub-directory	Typical contents
02-FIN	00-ARCHIVE	Old files for reference, including back-ups of company accounts from accounting software.
	01-ACCNTS	Each year's financial accounts and supporting material (such as monthly management accounts).
	02-VAT	VAT or equivalent.
	03-PURCHASES	Record of purchases by supplier.
	04-EMPEE EXPS	Records of employee expense claims (note these could also be filed under HR).
	05-CONTACTS	Directories for finance contacts such as accountant, advisors etc.
	06-RECORDS	Other financial records such as registration documents.
	07-INFO	Resources for the finance department, such as accounting news, tax news, finance articles etc.
	Example contributions to 01-DN shared folder	Employee expense claim form template. Purchase requisition template. Asset register.

Top directory	Sub-directory	Typical contents
03-HR	00-ARCHIVE	Old files for reference, including records from past members of staff and payroll software back-ups.
	01-CURRENT	Directory for each member of staff, with subfolders 0x-SURNAME, x being the payroll number, each folder then containing: 01-RECRUITMENT (recruitment records). 02-EMPLOY DOCS (contract records, contact details, performance appraisals, holiday records, pension details). 03-TIMESHEETS & PAYSLIPS. 04-PAYE DOCS (tax-related documents termed in the UK as Pay as you Earn). 05-TRAINING (records of courses, eg, first-aid training). 06-PHOTOS (for use in publicity). 07-GEN CORRES (other correspondence).
	02-PIPELINE	Sub-folders for each person in the recruitment process. This can also include work-experience placements.
	03-PAYE	General PAYE documents relating to the company rather than individual staff members, eg, monthly and yearly company returns or summaries.
	04-CONTACTS	Sub-folders of contacts relevant to this department, eg, schools, colleges, training providers, HR consultants, payroll service providers etc.
	05-INFO	Resources for the HR department, such as HR articles, employment law updates etc.
	Example contributions to 01-DN shared folder	Template for staff employment contract. Staff handbook (of staff policies). Company organization chart. Staff contact directory. Staff induction template. Staff-holiday record-sheet template. staff payslip template.

Top directory	Sub-directory	Typical contents
04-OPS	00-ARCHIVE	Old files for reference.
	01-IT	Software and hardware records including manuals, patches, updates, software license records, subscription details (eg, for cloud services).
	02-TRVL EVENTS	This could be included in other departments, such as FIN, HR, MKTG etc, but from experience it has been useful to have a separate folder in the OPS department as it multi-departmental and requires ticketing, hotels, events and so forth.
	03-LEGAL	This folder relates to general agreements and legal issues, but is usually only needed where the company activities give rise to extraordinary amounts of legal documentation requiring a separate department. Otherwise, it might be best left under BRD. Sub-folders can include data protection, leases, licences etc.
	04-FACS	This folder relates to facilities and again may be best left under BRD until facilities becomes a significant activity (leases, purchases, maintenance etc), depending on the nature of your business.
	05-INFO	Resources for the OPS department such as IT news, travel alerts, legal bulletins, etc.
	Example contributions to 01-DN shared folder	Staff Travel template. Software and Hardware summary sheet(s). PAT (Portable Appliance Testing) template. PAT records sheet. Legal templates (Non-disclosure agreements, license agreements, consulting agreements, etc.).

Top directory	Sub-directory	Typical contents
05-MKTNG	00-ARCHIVE	Old files for reference.
	01-LOGO	Logo source files and versions in various formats and sizes for use. These may be made available in the 00-DOCS area for general use.
	02-WEBSITE	Sub-folders relating to the website: 01-DOMAINS (may be different from hosting, as often a business has several variants that redirect, and these need to be registered with details kept on file for renewal). 02-HOSTING (web hosting site, including internet service provider's details, renewals and logins to the administrator panel). 03-GRAPHICS (sources of graphics used, especially where stock photos have been purchased or used and details need to be maintained). 04-ANALYTICS (accounts such as Google Analytics and any management reports relating to the analysis of the website(s) such as search engine optimization etc.
	03-SOCIAL NTWKS	Sub-folders for the various social networking marketing services subscribed to by the company such as Twitter, Facebook, Instagram etc.
	04-CHANNELS	Sub-folders for other marketing channels (other than those above) such as newspapers, trade magazines, relevant networks etc. These subfolders could include email correspondence and general information (like report cards and circulation numbers).

05-PUBLICITY	For example, sub-folders for each year and further sub-folders relating to specific campaigns and press releases. There is some overlap here with the TRVL & EVENTS section in OPS, because events may derive publicity.
06-COLLATERAL	Sub-folders of various marketing materials such as pop-up banner stands, flyers, brochures, give-away gifts (like branded pens, notepads and mugs). The graphic designs, suppliers and orders can thus all be recorded.
07-PRSNS	Presentations such as company overviews and product presentations. Other presentations may also reside with specific events in OPS or with Board Meetings in BRD, so some care is required keeping track of them and who can see or make use of them.
08-CONTACTS	Department contacts including web designers, graphic designers, social media consultants, collateral suppliers etc.
09-OUR EVENTS	Not always appropriate, but if you are an event organizer or have various launch events, then a separate folder to keep track of them is useful.
10-INFO	Resources for the MKTNG department, such as general news articles, marketing trend pieces etc.
Example contributions to 01-DN shared folder	Logo templates. Brand handbook. Company document templates (letterheads, compliments slips, business cards, report cover sheet, etc). Company marketing templates (brochures, flyers, pop-ups etc.). Presentation templates.

Top directory	Sub-directory	Typical contents
06-BD	00-ARCHIVE	Old files for reference.
	01-CONTACTS	A series of sub-folders for each company where business development is underway. These could be further separated into categories, such as funding, joint venture, production, sales etc. Other departments may then need shared access as appropriate.
	02-INFO	Resources for the BD department, such as industry news, overseas export market news etc.
	Example contributions to 01-DN shared folder	Prospective customer report templates.

Top directory	Sub-directory	Typical contents
07-SALES	00-ARCHIVE	Old files for reference.
	01-CONTACTS	Sub-folders for each sales contract by customer with associated correspondence, negotiation records and project details as appropriate.
	02-INFO	Resources for the SALES department, such as industry news, customer news etc.
	Example contributions to 01-DN shared folder	Product catalogue. Price list.

Top directory	Sub-directory	Typical contents
08-PROD	00-ARCHIVE	Old files for reference.
	01-PRODUCTS	Sub-folders of each product line and product runs with design specifications, bill-of-materials batch records, quality control and recall information.
	02-EQPT	Sub-folders for each item of equipment on the production line for example, including supplier, maintenance, calibration and service records.
	03-CONTACTS	Sub-folders for each contact, eg, materials or component supplier, equipment supplier (not included above), maintenance provider etc.
	04-INFO	Resources for the PROD department, such as industry news, competitor information consumer legislation, etc.
	Example contributions to 01-DN shared folder	Product data sheets. Product instruction manuals.

Top directory	Sub-directory	Typical contents
09-R&D	00-ARCHIVE	Old files for reference.
	01-PATENTS	Sub-folders of each invention disclosure, patent draft, patent pending or patent family going through grant.
	02-PROJECTS	Sub-folders for each R&D project with results, reports and developments.
	03-EQPT	Sub-folders for each item of equipment on the production line for example, including supplier, maintenance, calibration and service records.
	04-CONTACTS	Sub-folders for each contact, for example materials or component supplier, equipment supplier (not included above), collaborator (such as a university department) etc.
	05-INFO	Resources for the R&D department, such as industry news, general R&D information etc.
	Example contributions to 01-DN shared folder	Invention disclosure template. Patent drafting template.

Top directory	Sub-directory	Typical contents
10-INFO	Ad hoc	Companywide resources such as company news, industry news, white papers, etc. If it is department specific, then it would be placed in the respective INFO directory of the department.

APPENDIX B

PRESS RELEASE ON SINGULAR ID'S EXIT

Bilcare buys Singular ID as it plays out its strategy to become the leading anti-counterfeiting solution provider in the pharmaceutical industry

Singapore, 7th January 2008 – Singular ID, the provider of the integrated high technology enterprise brand security system called *enxure*, announced today that during December 2007 it was acquired by Bilcare Singapore Pte Ltd for SGD 19.58 million.

Bilcare Singapore is a wholly owned subsidiary of Bilcare Limited, a leading pharmaceutical packaging company offering research services, clinical services and packaging materials to hundreds of global customers. Bilcare is listed on the Mumbai Stock Exchange in India.

Singular ID spun off from the Institute of Materials Research and Engineering, Singapore in June 2005, and with venture-capital backing has grown to operate out of Singapore and Italy, delivering award-winning technology to customers in the fashion and automotive sectors.

Following the acquisition, the founding directors of Singular ID, Dr Adrian Burden and Dr Peter Moran, will continue to hold positions on the Board and to run the company as chief executive officer and chief technology officer respectively.

'This acquisition by a strong corporate entity is excellent news for Singular ID and its first rate team,' stated Dr Burden. 'We are now in a position to work as part of a global leader in the pharmaceutical sector to tackle the problem of counterfeit medicines and create a real impact in this high-volume business. In addition, Bilcare has aligned with our vision to be the de facto anti-counterfeiting and track-and-trace solution provider in a number of key sectors, and so we remain committed to build significant value in our business beyond the pharmaceutical sector.'

Bilcare has publicized its interest in anti-counterfeiting technology previously, having developed a number of packaging solutions in-house and formed strategic alliances with companies. However, this acquisition underlines the importance that Bilcare places on offering state-of-the-art anti-counterfeiting solutions, particularly fully integrated systems such as Singular ID's *enxure* product. It also indicates how important the issues of brand protection are to the pharmaceutical and medical industry.

Dr Peter Moran comments: 'We have already been interacting with Bilcare's technical teams in both Singapore and India and can see great potential and synergy arising from this transaction. Bilcare brings important manufacturing experience that will help us to quickly scale up our production to meet the requirements of very high-volume, very low-item cost, and yet robust security. As we achieve this for pharmaceutical applications, we will be able to apply this to our other target sectors and provide an even more competitive product.'

Joining the Board of Singular ID will be Dr Rahul Bharadia, director of research at Bilcare Singapore, Mr Vineet Mehrotra, vice-president (finance) of Bilcare, and Mr Mohan H. Bhandari the chairman and managing director of Bilcare.

'With counterfeit medicines affecting the safety of the consumer, as well as damaging the reputation and bottom line of the pharmaceutical industry, there is a real need for a scalable and robust solution. I am delighted to have brought Singular ID into the Bilcare group and to add the *enxure* system to our future product line', explained Mr Bhandari.

About Singular ID Pte Ltd

Headquartered in Singapore, and with a subsidiary in Padua, northern Italy, Singular ID is a technology company engaged in research, development and creation of micro and nanotechnology based novel products. With a mission to safeguard customers' interests by providing integrated tagging solutions, Singular ID is a leading solution provider for tracing and authenticating items of value. Singular ID has a customer-centric approach and works closely with its clients to tailor its technology to meet specific customer requirements. Singular ID has licensed core technology from the Agency for Science Technology and Research (A*STAR), Singapore.

About Bilcare

Headquartered in India, Bilcare provides integrated packaging solutions across the pharmaceutical value chain through its key business activities; pharma-packaging research, global clinical services and research academy. Bilcare operates state-of-the-art manufacturing and research facilities in India, Singapore, US and UK, and has regional offices in Brazil, Germany, China and Australia, which cater to global clients including J&J, Merck, GSK, Sanofi, Aventis, Pfizer, Novartis, Wyeth, Ranbaxy and Dr. Reddy's. Bilcare partners with the global pharmaceutical sector by providing value solutions to address their key concerns viz. counterfeit, compliance, cost communication and convenience.

ACKNOWLEDGMENTS

Particular thanks go to Peter Moran with whom I shared the journey from start to exit in Singular ID. We would not have achieved it without his humour, attention to fine print and engineering excellence. Thanks also to Albert Yee, Mike Loh and Lim Khiang Wee for smoothing the way for the Institute of Materials Research and Engineering's first spin-out company. I also thank Matthias Andermatt and Gabriela Sidler for their optimism during this period, and Wolfram Schiweck for his meticulous approach to patent drafting and patent portfolio management. Thanks also go to Stefano Gallucci for his support in Italy as we navigated the waters of starting and growing our first overseas subsidiary.

I also acknowledge Pete Dobson for his support over many years as we both became involved in different technology start-ups and shared both frustrations and insights.

My first experience in a venture capital funded start-up was as an employee in the team at Printable Field Emitters. Thank you to Ravi Silva for alerting me to the job opportunity and to Andy Harding, Richard Tuck, Bill Taylor and Peter Jones for that exciting ride during the formative years of my career.

In Singapore I had the chance to lead a number of business and technology roadmapping exercises, learning the methodology from Robert Phaal, Chris Holmes and Mike Ferrill. This provided invaluable insights into a broad range of smaller companies and how they were each managing the process of scaling up.

I mention Tom Alcott as my latest business partner as we embark together on a blockchain technology start-up, looking forward to the exit in a few years.

Thanks to Adam Jolly for patiently working with me through the drafts of the manuscript, providing helpful feedback and much encouragement to finish the task at hand.

And finally, of course, I thank Emma with whom I have a family, innovation centre, business consultancy and two social enterprises. I suspect she wishes she had done more due diligence before we married.

Printed in Great Britain
by Amazon